WHALES

Touching the Mystery

DOUG THOMPSON

NEWSAGE PRESS
Troutdale, Oregon

WHALES: *Touching the Mystery*

Book and DVD Copyright © 2006 by Doug Thompson
Paperback Original ISBN 0-939165-55-4

AUTHOR'S NOTE: I have chosen to capitalize the names of all whale species written about in this book out of respect for the whales. I understand that the scientific approach to taxonomy is to lower case whale species, however, as a naturalist who approaches the whales as individuals and families, I want to honor them.

NEWSAGE PRESS
PO Box 607
Troutdale, OR 97060-0607
503-695-2211
www.newsagepress.com

Front Cover Design by Doug Thompson, Sherry Wachter, and David S. Miller. Back cover design by Sherry Wachter. Illustration adapted from the art of J.D. Mayhew. Book Design by Sherry Wachter.

Printed in the United States
Distributed in the United States and Canada by
Publishers Group West 800-788-3123

Library of Congress cataloging-in-Publication Data

Thompson, Doug, 1947-
  Whales : touching the mystery / Doug Thompson.
    p. cm.
  Includes index.
  ISBN-13: 978-0-939165-55-1 (alk. paper)
  ISBN-10: 0-939165-55-4 (alk. paper)
  1. Gray whale–Behavior–Mexico–Baja California (Peninsula) 2. Whale watching–Mexico–Baja California (Peninsula) 3. Human-animal relationships–Mexico–Baja California (Peninsula) 4. Whaling 5. Endangered species I. Title.
QL737.C425T46 2006
599.5--dc22

                                                        2006025424
            1 2 3 4 5 6 7 8 9 10

To Robin
a friend to all of nature

⤙⤚

Why do whales living wild and free in the ocean,

seek encounters with humans? Doug Thompson shares

his thirty years of experience studying gray whales in remote

Baja, Mexico lagoons, and with his book and DVD

explores the mystery of this extraordinary interspecies connection.

And he shares, too, his love for the whales, the place, and the people.

It is an inspiring story, and illustrates how conservation of wild life,

the economic well being of the local people, and the

often life-changing experience of those who become involved

are, together, weaving a message of hope for the

future of the whales – and for us all.

JANE GOODALL, PhD, DBE
UN Messenger of Peace

Acknowledgments

This book became reality because of three extraordinary women, and I am deeply grateful to each of them. Brenda Peterson, author and friend, can call dolphins and whales to a boat in a most magical way. Brenda introduced me to Maureen R. Michelson, publisher of NewSage Press. Maureen's support, guidance, and understanding of a first time author is proof of someone following her passion. Maureen's skills as a writer, editor, and researcher have been invaluable in bringing this book to fruition. And my wonderful wife, Robin Kobaly, has an unwavering belief in me that gave me the courage to bring this dream to reality. Robin's incredible photographs and discerning eye captured in images the story of San Ignacio Lagoon and the magnificent Gray Whales.

Taking the raw materials of text and photographs, and creating a handsome book demands the special talent and creativity of a book designer. I am grateful to NewSage Press's book designer, Sherry Wachter, for her talent and creative vision. I would also like to acknowledge Tracy Smith of NewSage Press for her editing skills in the final stages of the manuscript. And in the early drafts of my book, Caroline Conway offered suggestions and help. I am grateful to our daughter, Holly, who in the final hours was a great help with proofing. A special thanks to Dave Miller for his production talents as a camera man for the DVD, and as a map maker for the book.

As a young man I met many wonderful people who cared about the whales. In particular I want to acknowledge the late James D. (JD) and Noretta Mayhew for their friendship, our travels, their dedication and hard work in initiating the Mendocino Whale War, and for their overall enthusiasm for whales until they died. I am particularly grateful for JD's inspiring marine artwork that graces this book, and for giving me permission years ago to use his art to help promote the awareness of whales. I think JD would be pleased.

I was fortunate to have as a friend the late, great Byrd Baker of Mendocino, who championed the whales' cause when it was not popular. He was a fine warrior for the good of all whales. I owe Tony DiScala for taking in a novice on his commercial fishing boat the *El Sole* and teaching me about the ocean when I was a young man. Tony was my lifelong pal.

For my dear friend and surfing pal, Steve Wood, a special thanks for all the paddle-outs, even when it's blown-out and small. Our talks between sets are as inspiring as his music. I would also like to thank Gary McAvoy for many years of celebrations.

Special thanks to the adventurers who had the vision years ago to take people to a remote area in Baja to see wild whales: Dennis Bostic and Margery Stinson, Peter Ott—explorer extraordinaire, Frank LoPreste, and the people of Fisherman's Landing in San Diego. The captains and crews of the *Searcher, The Royal Polaris, The Royal Star* were all there in the beginning of whale watching in Baja.

Muchas gracias to Ranulfo Mayoral of San Ignacio Lagoon for his friendship and for sharing his vast knowledge of the lagoon and the whales. I am also grateful to Pachico and Carmen Mayoral for their friendship. A special thanks to marine biologist José Ángel Sánchez Pacheco for that inspirational drive in the R.V. down through Baja when we brainstormed over the idea for *Instituto SummerTree*. It is now a reality. José is a good friend and a man who loves the Gray Whales, and Baja, with all of its natural wonders.

And to the wonderful people of San Ignacio Lagoon, *muchas gracias* for opening your hearts and homes, particularly in the making of the book and the DVD. You have paradise and you know it.

Lastly, my unending gratitude to the Gray Whales of San Ignacio Lagoon—they changed my life forever.

DOUG THOMPSON
July 2006

Contents

WHALES
Touching the Mystery

Doug Thompson greets a Gray Whale in San Ignacio Lagoon.

INTRODUCTION

A Calling from the Whales

When I began leading whale watching trips as a young man in 1977, I did not realize my life would be so profoundly affected by San Ignacio Lagoon, the whales, and the local people. The day I had my first physical contact with a Gray Whale, the lagoon was calm and the warm sun soothing. I had five people in our sixteen-foot, aluminum skiff, which we launched from our ninety-five-foot vessel, *The Searcher*. We had just anchored after a two-day trip from San Diego.

As we slowly cruised within the mouth of the lagoon, whales were breaching, spy hopping, and spouting. Sometimes they would get within fifteen or twenty feet of our skiff. This alone was thrilling. Then it happened. A mother whale and her baby began to circle our skiff, coming closer with each pass. We kicked our small outboard engine into neutral so the prop was not moving. We knew it was a good idea to have the engine running to let the whales know where we were in their acoustic world. After about ten minutes, the mother slowly headed straight toward our skiff with her baby by her side. Every historic account I had ever read warned that a boat caught between a mother and her baby was dangerous. We did not engage the prop for fear of hurting the whales. Everyone looked at me and I realized I had no idea what was going to happen next. I flashed on the thought, *All these people have signed up for this trip after hearing me give a presentation*

1

on whales. I did describe the trip as an adventure, but I never said or thought it might be dangerous.

Now we were within arm's length of a full-grown mother whale about forty-five feet long and weighing some sixty thousand pounds, and her two-thousand pound baby. Just then the mom stopped next to the port side of our skiff and the baby moved just off the stern with his head almost in the skiff. Everyone waited for me to say something, do something. Even the mother whale, her massive body right next to the boat with her head tilted up, looked at me expectantly. Within moments I decided, *This way of dying is far better than being flattened by a car on the freeway.*

I reached out and touched the mother. She submerged a little and then came right back up, seeming to want more. So, following my heart, I reached out and tried to hug her. It was pretty hard to hug the whale, but I gave it a good try. Everyone in the skiff had been sitting motionless, watching in silence. Then, as if deciding within moments that it was safe, they moved to the sides of the skiff and began stroking the mother and the baby.

After awhile we looked up at one another. We all had tears in our eyes. This was a surreal world we had entered—one where two unlikely species reached out to one another. Touching and hugging whales in the wild did not fit into our realities, yet there we were communing with the whales! In turn, the whales seemed aware of just how vulnerable we were, and they were careful not to rock the boat or move us around too much. We had stroked and touched the mom and baby for a good twenty minutes when I realized we had drifted about a mile from *The Searcher* in this remote desert lagoon. The encounter ended when the mom moved about ten feet away from the skiff and somehow signaled her baby that playtime with the humans was over. The baby then moved next to mom and off they went.

While motoring back to *The Searcher,* everyone began talking at once, yet we could not quite express what we were thinking and feeling. Somehow we had slipped into another dimension and we were not sure what to make of this. No one took photos even though we all had good camera gear with us in the skiff. By the end of our stay that season, everyone on board had a friendly encounter with a whale. And every trip after that, it just got better.

This was not the first time I had come eye-to-eye with a great Gray Whale. Some fifteen years before that first trip to San Ignacio Lagoon, a chance encounter bound my life to the world of whales. I was thirteen years old, surfing off the coast of Huntington Beach, California. On that particular day it was unusually calm, and I had been waiting for quite awhile to catch a decent wave. Finally, I felt a swell and turned to look for the wave that might carry me to shore. Suddenly a huge spout of warm, pungent water blasted through the glassy sea and sprayed me. Startled, but too fascinated to be scared, I sat motionless while this whale, maybe forty feet long, surfaced. She forcefully sucked in air through two blowholes the size of saucers. This was my first time hearing a whale breath,

Eye of a Gray Whale

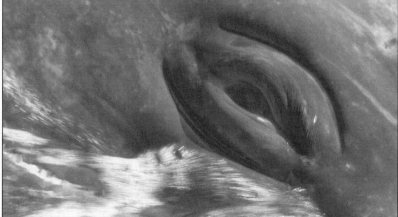

ROBIN KOBALY

3

a sound I would never forget. Then the whale rolled slightly to one side and looked straight at me with her deep, dark eye the size of a softball. In that moment all thought, and time itself, disappeared. I held my breath and stared back, face-to-face with a Gray Whale. After what seemed like a long time, she pumped her tail slowly, turned in a half circle, and glided away. I was alone again, and despite my youth somehow I knew I would never be the same.

That day was the beginning of a relationship with whales and the ocean that has lasted my entire life. Nearly every meaningful lesson I have ever learned and every inspiring person I have ever met, has been because of my connection with whales. The quest to learn more about whales has led me on many adventures to international waters—from New Zealand to Hawaii to Alaska, and most important, along the Pacific coastline of North America following the Gray Whales. I am a whale enthusiast of sorts, convinced these creatures can transform the way we humans live. They certainly have changed my life, and it is my passion to share the excitement of being in the presence of one of earth's grandest creatures.

Some people have been privileged to enter the world of another species. Jane Goodall with the chimpanzees and Farley Mowat with the wolves immediately come to mind. Each altered their way of living to better fit the rhythm of their chosen species, and each was fundamentally changed in the process. As a result they garnered tremendous insight into the worlds and intelligences of other species. These insights have enriched human understanding and appreciation of other animals.

These individuals have been a tremendous inspiration to me in my own efforts to enter the world of the whales. Though I have not been able to live in the whales' world for extended periods of time, I have witnessed and experienced friendly, interspecies interactions between

4

whales and humans for thirty years. I have been privileged to know others who have studied the whales, or who have lived their whole lives on the shores of San Ignacio's Baja birthing lagoon. And I have spent time with thousands of whale watchers whose lives have been changed simply by the sight or the touch of whales. They have all taught me many things about the whales, and about being human.

What I now know without a doubt is that whales demonstrate a profound intelligence and social capability far beyond what humans previously have considered. Just because we do not understand whales, their languages, or their cultures does not mean these do not exist. Humans simply have yet to extensively study or comprehend the world of whales. Science knows little about them, but this does not give us the right to dismiss the whales' importance until we can "scientifically" prove their significance or intelligence. It will take generations to unravel many of the mysteries that surround a whale's life. In the meantime, we must figure out a way to co-exist with them, respectfully, and ensure that whales have a secure future on the planet.

I have written this book to share the wondrous world of whales as well as to heighten people's awareness of modern threats encroaching on whales and the oceans. Every year I follow the Gray Whale migrations apprehensively, wondering how many will make the journey safely from their Baja birthing lagoons to the Arctic feeding grounds. At times I am astonished and saddened by the obstacles we humans place in their paths: lethal underwater sonar testing, shipping lane threats, the ravages of overfishing with nets, toxic pollutants, and the growing fallout from global warming. Their watery world is at great risk.

For most of the last nine hundred years, humans have hunted whales commercially. To this day there are a few rogue nations that continue to hunt whales despite protests from the majority of countries. As of mid-2006 the debate over resuming international whaling has heated up. In this new century the majority of cultures worldwide understand that whales are of much greater value alive than dead. However, some countries still see whale hunting as a viable industry, particularly as some whale populations rebound. What I see in this new century for whales and humans is a grand opportunity for humans to make livelihoods from *watching* the whales rather than *hunting* them. And beyond the economic discussion, whales offer humans emotional, psychological, and spiritual wealth—unquantifiable riches that could extend far into the future.

We have assailed the whales with different threats for hundreds of years—chasing some species of whales to the brink of extinction. Yet despite it all, in the last couple of decades the whales have been trying to make friendly contact with humans. What we do with this in the near future could mean the beginning or the end of this remarkable relationship between whales and humans. We face a tremendous challenge and opportunity to find ways to share the oceans with the whales. I hope this book will further the discussion on how to live side-by-side with the whales—to find ways to share the earth more magnanimously. Then there will be room for the mysteries of the whales to unfold.

Gray Whale fluke

ROBIN KOBALY

PART ONE

Laguna San Ignacio

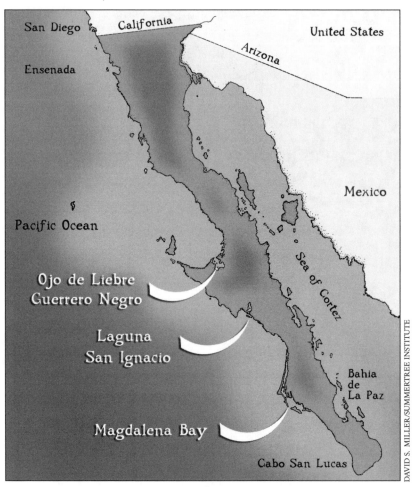

San Diego
California
United States

Ensenada

Arizona

Mexico

Pacific Ocean

Sea of Cortez

Ojo de Liebre
Guerrero Negro

Laguna
San Ignacio

Bahia
de
La Paz

Magdalena Bay

Cabo San Lucas

Map of Baja

ONE

Where Whales and Humans Meet

*N*o matter how many times I fly into the small dirt airstrip along San Ignacio Lagoon, I feel the excitement of a kid coming home. From the window of the small airplane the outline of the lagoon loosely resembles the shape of a whale, its glimmering, pale sapphire waters surrounded on three sides by sun-bleached desert and white salt flats. Purplish-brown mountain ranges in the distance crown the lagoon and its stark landscape. From the air the lagoon looks placid and almost delicate under Baja's intense sunlight, seemingly incapable of holding hundreds of whales and their newborns. But every year migrating Gray Whales return to these home waters to mate and birth.

San Ignacio Lagoon or *Laguna San Ignacio* is a touchstone for me, a pilgrimage I have made almost every year since 1976—by boat, car, or plane. In these waters both whales and humans can rest, reveling in the playful antics of baby whales and the tender protectiveness of their mothers. This remote, flat terrain offers unobstructed views of sunrises, sunsets, and moonrises. And on clear moonless nights, stars crowd the black Baja skies, free from human-made light. This pristine and safe environment makes it possible for human and whale alike to gain strength for future journeys.

As we descend toward the isolated dirt runway adjacent to the lagoon, long shadowy whale shapes glide just beneath the water's surface.

A familiar rush of relaxation and anticipation settles over me. Once again I will greet the returning whales as well as local families who have lived on the lagoon's shores for years. This is also the time of year when I welcome new whale watchers who will share in the mystery of the Gray Whales.

Approaching Gray Whale mother and baby

The Gray Whales

The Eastern Pacific Gray Whales, or *Eschrichtius robustus,* begin arriving at San Ignacio Lagoon in mid-December, returning from their Arctic summer feeding grounds. They travel south along the Pacific Coastline from the Bering, Chukchi, and North Pacific Seas to the warm waters of Baja some four to five thousand miles away. The Gray Whale migration is among the longest migratory routes known for a mammal, averaging about five thousand miles each way.

By mid-January San Ignacio Lagoon is once again alive with hundreds of whales and their babies. These leviathans can be as big as 45 to nearly 50 feet in length and on average weigh twenty-five tons or more, if pregnant. A newborn Gray Whale can weigh close to two thousand pounds and average about fifteen feet in length. In the first weeks the calves stay close to their protective and affectionate mothers, drinking about thirty to fifty gallons of their mothers' fat-laden milk on a daily basis. This translates into a daily weight gain of up to fifty pounds. This Baja respite for the whales serves as a protected environment for calving as well as for mating before the Gray Whales once again make their journey north through potentially dangerous seas, especially for young whales.

Baja Birthing Lagoons

Other prominent Gray Whale birthing lagoons of Baja include *Guerrero Negro* and *Ojo de Liebre,* which are connected to one another by a small, intermittently shallow channel that runs through a marsh between the two lagoons. *Laguna San Ignacio* is further to the south and beyond that is *Bahia Magdalena.* All of these lagoons and a few other smaller ones are home to the Eastern Pacific Gray Whales. It is in these lagoons, and especially at *Laguna San Ignacio,* that "friendly whales" or *ballenas amistosas* seek out humans for interaction. The first known friendly contact between a Gray Whale and a human in San Ignacio Lagoon happened in February 1972. The remarkable interaction between a frightened yet courageous fisherman, Francisco "Pachico" Mayoral, and a trusting friendly Gray Whale was the beginning of a unique relationship that now draws thousands of visitors to Baja birthing lagoons every spring.

San Ignacio is the only Baja lagoon off limits to commercial vessels, salt barges, and other large-scale noise and pollution. The 37,560-acre lagoon is relatively shallow with the deepest channel in the lagoon averaging fifty to sixty feet deep. In 2006 Ranulfo Mayoral, Pachico's son, and a local fisherman and naturalist, used an eco-sounder or "fish finder" to identify an area near the lagoon's mangroves that is ninety-four-feet deep. The lagoon's deep channel is ideal for whales traveling its length for mating, birthing, and preparing their young for the northern migration.

Many consider San Ignacio to be the most natural and undisturbed Gray Whale migration destination on earth. It is designated as a UNESCO World Heritage Site, and a Ramsar site, which means San Ignacio Lagoon is a wetland of international importance because of its large population of migratory birds. San Ignacio Lagoon is also part of El Vizcaíno Biosphere Reserve, Mexico's second largest protected area. But despite this international recognition, the future protection of San Ignacio is an ongoing process with efforts and negotiations continuing among the local residents, environmentalists, and the Mexican government.

Whale Watching

Regulations for San Ignacio Lagoon allow whale watching primarily in January, February, March, and April, although permits can be issued as early as December. Ecotourism groups hire local fishers, who use their twenty to twenty-four foot *pangas* (skiffs) for whale watching. These *pangas* comfortably seat six to seven people with a limit of ten, and allow for close contact with friendly whales. The local residents know the importance of taking great care to keep San Ignacio a safe haven for the whales, birds, and other natural resources while at the same time providing for their families with ecotourism and an ongoing fishing business. In many ways San Ignacio Lagoon is an excellent example of how a local community can thrive economically while at the same time protecting its natural resources for future generations.

By mid-May the last of the whales will depart from Baja for their northern migration, most of them reaching the rich, subpolar waters

Reddish Egret in mangroves of San Ignacio Lagoon

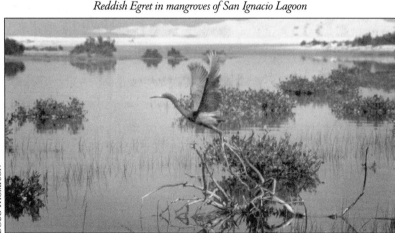

DOUG THOMPSON

of the Chukchi and Bering Seas. A handful of whales may stay in Baja waters or points further north year-round, however most head for the feeding grounds in Arctic seas. Gray Whales primarily eat amphipods, small bottom-dwelling creatures, usually under an inch long. Their huge baleen mouths suck up the sand and mud from the sea floor and filter out all but the amphipods and other small creatures. How ironic that some of earth's largest animals, the baleen whales, feed on some of earth's smallest creatures. A Gray Whale can eat about sixty-seven tons of food while feasting in the Arctic's sub-polar feeding grounds, rejuvenating their fat supplies for the trip home. In early October when the Arctic days shorten and northern waters begin to freeze, the Gray Whales once again begin their journey home to Baja.

The Landscape

Laguna San Ignacio is located on the Pacific Coast of Baja California Sur, Mexico, about six hundred miles south of the Mexico-U.S. border. Intertidal mudflats, salt flats, sand dunes, mangrove marshes, and a plant-dotted coastal plain intersected by densely vegetated *arroyos* weave together to create this stark yet breathtaking landscape that frames the lagoon. With the Pacific Ocean to the west, and mountain ranges—*Sierra de Santa Clara, Sierra de San Francisco,* and *Sierra de Guadalupe*—to the east, south, and north, San Ignacio sits like a rare jewel, or what environmentalists refer to as a "biogem."

This desert environment sustains sturdy plants such as copal, mesquite, galloping cactus, mallow, sunflowers, fishhook cactus, and jojoba—all of which thrive in this salty arid land. During whale watching season the only regular moisture comes from morning dew or an evening coastal marine layer. A sporadic rain will drench the desert floor, always bringing new life.

Right next to the parched desert landscape are extensive wetlands in and around the lagoon, providing rich feeding grounds and habitat for nearly two hundred bird species. The amount of life and life-giving nutrients in these waters is extraordinarily high, capable of supporting an amazing variety of plants and animals. In addition, salt-tolerant mangrove trees thrive here. Hundreds of acres of thick red mangrove *(Rhizophora mangle)* and white mangrove *(Languncularia racemosa)* forests stretch along the lagoon shoreline for miles, congregating in the natural water channels of low-lying areas. The mangroves along with the wetlands and beaches of San Ignacio are extremely important for

San Ignacio Lagoon with Sierra de Santa Clara *range to the northwest*

ROBIN KOBALY

ROBIN KOBALY

Mangrove tree in San Ignacio Lagoon with
Sierra de Santa Clara *range to the northwest*

shorebirds and the various waterfowl of the Pacific Flyway. This is one
of the most important flying routes for hundreds of thousands of birds
migrating from Alaska to Mexico, and some as far as South America.
The lagoon landscape also provides critical habitat for rare species such
as peregrine falcons and osprey. San Ignacio Lagoon is a birder's wonder-
land as well as a whale watcher's.

Within these mangroves the seawater teams with fish that make
for good eating for humans and birds alike. Many species of fish begin
life in the shallow, protected waters of the mangroves among cordgrass,
saltwort, and pickleweed. Sierra, mullet, corvine, and snook are just a
sampling of the fish life within the thick mangroves. Once the fish are
big enough, they move to the open sea. Some fishers set gillnets across
the entrances to the mangrove inlets to catch mullet, stingray, and gui-
tarfish. Bat rays and sand sharks also reside in the lagoon, easily spotted
as they quickly glide and dart through shallow waters.

On a full moon with a high tide, kayakers can quietly glide through
narrow channels in the mangroves, hemmed in and protected by thousands of thick roots and limbs crisscrossed and entwined in a complex

union. This natural buffer from rough seas and high winds holds a calm and stillness that allow for spectacular bird watching. We often take night hikes to sit near the mangroves and listen to the wilderness rustling and calling out in the dark, unfettered by civilization and human intrusion.

Bottlenose Dolphins and green sea turtles live in the lagoon year round. The green sea turtle is listed as an endangered species worldwide, along with all seven species of sea turtles, including the Hawksbill, Kemp's Ridley, Olive Ridley, Loggerhead, Flatback, and Leatherback. Adult green sea turtles can be up to four feet in carapace length (the length of their shell) and can weigh as much as three to four hundred pounds. If you are lucky, you might see a green sea turtle pop up for a brief look while swimming in the lagoon.

During low tide, miles of shoreline are exposed, revealing tide pools teaming with sea life. Octopi, eels, sea horses, and an array of shellfish thrive in the sea rocks. The daily tide changes in the lagoon allow you to tune into the Earth's rhythms and observe the details of the constantly changing shoreline. Desert animals in the surrounding area include jackrabbits, bobcats, and coyotes. Mostly nocturnal, these animals take advantage of cooler temperatures and night to hunt. Occasionally, you might catch a glimpse of a lone coyote loping across white desert flats crusted with ancient black algal crust. Animals will often head for the shorelines at low tide to forage and scavenge for fish and dead sea animals.

Touching the Whales

In 1977 I led my first whale watching expedition to San Ignacio Lagoon. We traveled on *The Searcher,* a long-range vessel that departed from San Diego and arrived at San Ignacio Lagoon two days later. On that first excursion thirty-two excited whale watchers endured

DOUG THOMPSON

Friendly whale encounter in the 1970s

two days of rough seas for the opportunity to see the Gray Whales up close. I had heard about their friendly contact, but was not sure what to expect. That first day at the lagoon we launched sixteen-foot aluminum boats from *The Searcher* in order to get closer to the whales. At that time I did not know the local fishermen although I had heard about their friendly interactions with the Gray Whales. In the 1970s there were no regulations on whale watching in the lagoon, and only a small number of visitors made the arduous journey to the lagoon either by car or by boat.

On that first whale-watching trip in San Ignacio Lagoon there were a couple of hundred whales. Several were curious enough to approach our boat. We had a brief encounter and actually got to touch a whale. The following year I led another trip for whale watchers and this time maybe twenty curious whales approached our boat

ROBIN KOBALY

A baby Gray Whale lays on her side to see the human during friendly contact.

for friendly interaction. On our trip to the lagoon in 1979 we met many friendly whales, and were assured of an encounter almost every time we went out in a *panga*. Every year after that, friendly whale interactions have steadily increased.

The only reason I can offer for such a dramatic change in behavior with the whales over such a short time period is that the whales had to be communicating with one another. I believe they told each other it was now safe—the humans in the birthing lagoons were not going to hurt them. Around the same time friendly whale contact began in San Ignacio Lagoon it had also started in *Laguna Ojo de Liebre* to the north and *Bahia Magdalena* to the south. Interestingly, a year earlier the Mexican government had declared *Ojo de Liebre* the world's first whale sanctuary.

Since the 1970s the increase in friendly whale interactions has been dramatic. It was also in the 1970s that hunting of all whale species along the Pacific coast of North America ceased. The Gray Whale population steadily increased in numbers from near extinction of maybe a couple of thousand whales to between about eighteen to twenty thousand Gray Whales at the beginning of the twenty-first century.

Now Gray Whale mothers and babies routinely seek interaction with human visitors in Baja birthing lagoons. Their visits can easily last fifteen minutes or more, the whales floating on their sides to get a good look at the animated humans who stroke them and speak to them in sweet tones. Often, the whales let humans rub their baleen and thick tongues, basking in the massage.

Many times I have thought about the reasons behind the whales' friendly behavior. Perhaps humans and Gray Whales have re-established a relationship that existed long before whaling began. If we had decided not to slaughter whales for their resources, but instead decided to respect their right to coexist with humans, would the friendly interaction between whales and humans be a worldwide phenomenon?

I believe the Gray Whales are trying to share something important with us through their touch and closeness. After three decades of such meetings with the Gray Whales of San Ignacio I often wonder, *What if this contact with whales has been possible all along and we have simply chosen fear and short-sighted greed over relationship?* Maybe it is we humans who have finally made contact—and the whales have been waiting. I now think of San Ignacio as the lagoon of forgiveness. Perhaps the whales are forgiving us for nearly hunting them to extinction.

A friendly exchange in San Ignacio Lagoon

TWO

Between Whales and Humans

hat a San Ignacio fisherman discovered in 1972 has changed the way we perceive whales in this new millennium. Francisco "Pachico" Mayoral was the first person known to touch a Gray Whale in a friendly interaction. At that time people still considered Gray Whales to be "devil fish" capable of harming humans if they got too close. In some ways Pachico's interspecies connection with the Gray Whales is similar to what Jane Goodall accomplished with chimpanzees in the jungles of Gombe. Each human slowly glimpsed a more accurate view of another species' world, ultimately reshaping our view of and behavior toward those animals.

Jane Goodall taught us that if we unobtrusively enter the world of another species as passive observers, we discover that they are capable of behaviors and communication we humans never imagined. In the case of Gray Whales, Pachico Mayoral had been a part of the world of San Ignacio Lagoon for years, innately knowing the life and moods of this isolated inlet off the Pacific Ocean. When observing the whales, Pachico did not intrude, and he went out of his way to keep his distance from the whales. It was in this passive role that Pachico observed and finally experienced friendly behavior that would have seemed impossible just years earlier. Gray Whales have been hunted to near extinction twice by humans, with the entire Atlantic population decimated. Yet the whales seek friendly interaction with humans. This contact between Gray Whales and humans is miraculous.

Many adult whales alive today also were alive in the 1970s and earlier at a time when humans killed whales. Gray Whales are now thought to live seventy-five to one hundred years or more. It is conceivable that an older mother whale migrating to San Ignacio Lagoon in 2006 might remember a time when whalers hunted along the Pacific coastline. Possibly there is a harpoon scar running along the whale's side. And yet here she is, alongside our boat, trusting humans to touch her newborn. It seems as if these long-lived creatures have somehow forgiven us—as if we have been given a second chance.

The First Friendly Touch

One February morning while Pachico was working with his fishing partner, Santo Luis Perez, a Gray Whale approached their eighteen-foot, wooden *panga*. As the whale swam closer, Pachico tried to move the *panga* away from the whale, but she kept surfacing next to the boat. The whale eventually got under the *panga*, and Pachico had no other option but to stay still. He felt both fear and exhilaration not knowing what this whale was doing. When Pachico tells the story he says, "All I knew was a big animal double the size of my *panga* was now in charge."

With a gentleness that belied her great size, the whale gently rubbed against the boat. As Pachico watched, his fear began to melt. At one point the whale raised her head a couple of feet out of the water right in front of Pachico, perhaps to get a better look at the humans. The two fishermen watched, uncertain what to do. In that moment Pachico made a great leap of trust and timidly reached out. With one finger he quickly

ROBIN KOBALY

Pachico greets a Gray Whale.

touched the whale's mammoth head. The whale did not pull away, but instead moved closer to Pachico. Then he realized he could stroke the whale and began to pet her sleek head, speckled with sprouts of hair, barnacles, and whale lice. The whale seemed to enjoy the exchange, and Pachico was both surprised and delighted. That day the world shifted for Pachico—and perhaps for the Gray Whales of San Ignacio, too.

When Pachico and Santo returned to their fishing village with this incredible story, people found it hard to believe and thought maybe Pachico had lost his mind. Never before had there been a friendly encounter with a whale in the lagoon. The locals discussed this important event at length over the next several days. They asked one another, "What does it mean to have the whales approaching our boats? Are the whales changing? Could this happen again? What should we do the next time?" For generations everyone in the village had always been concerned about getting too close to the whales. In the past fishermen would knock on the sides of their *pangas* in an effort to scare off any approaching whales.

Pachico started taking friends out into the lagoon to show them his story was true. Then friends told their friends, and this is how Pachico began his first whale watching outings. In time, other fishers began to have similar experiences with friendly whales.

From Devil Fish to Friendly Whales

Before Pachico's first friendly exchange with a Gray Whale, local fishermen were too fearful to get close to the whales and certainly avoided getting between a mother and baby. They generally avoided whales, familiar with the stories about the "hard-headed devil fish" who turned on the whalers when they threatened the babies in the lagoon. Gray Whale mothers fought ferociously to protect their babies, smashing the whalers' skiffs that relentlessly pursued the whales into the birthing lagoons, turning the waters red with the whales' blood. Years later after the hunting stopped, visitors and local fishermen alike kept a respectable distance from the whales.

Within a couple years of Pachico's first contact, the villagers' long-held beliefs about fierce whales and their aggressive behavior faded, and they began to share new stories about *ballenas amistosas* (friendly whales). A new relationship had begun between humans and whales at San Ignacio Lagoon. This incredible event, though much talked about in the fishing village, was little known outside of their isolated lagoon for a couple of years.

Before then no one had reported friendly physical contact between the Gray Whales and humans. Scientists, biologists, early environmentalists, and a handful of adventurous whale watchers who visited the Baja lagoons from the 1950s on, described the whales in numerous ways—from outright "unsocial" to "almost within touching distance." But no one claimed they had touched a Gray Whale. All of that changed when Pachico reached out.

Eye-to-Eye with Whales

Now thousands of whale watchers make the long journey to Baja birthing lagoons to experience the *ballenas amistosas*. About five thousand tourists visit San Ignacio Lagoon each year during whale watching season, some staying the day, others staying a week or more. On a typical day in San Ignacio, *panga* drivers take visitors to a designated whale-watching area near the mouth of the lagoon. The trained boat drivers are careful not to pursue the whales, but make their *pangas* available for interested whales seeking contact. It is likely that sooner or later a Gray Whale mother will allow her baby to approach a *panga* and the fun begins. The first encounter with whales can be startling as you watch a forty-foot, thirty-ton whale accompanied by her two-ton baby swim straight toward the *panga*—and a great relief to see them easily pull up alongside the boat for a friendly exchange. It can be equally startling when a mother whale gently scratches her barnacled head along the bottom of the boat, slightly nudging or lifting it out of the water. Boat drivers call this "hugging the boat."

Baby Gray Whales enjoy having their baleen and tongues rubbed.

LINDA YAPP

During these friendly encounters, babies and mothers allow humans to rub their heads mottled with white barnacles and yellowish whale lice. Their rostrums, or upper jaws, are dimpled with thick individual hairs. A baby can pop his sleek body out of the water far enough for a human to hug him, and maybe even plant a kiss. Whales often roll their bodies to the side to get a good look at their visitors. A whale's eyes are located far back on the head, just beyond the corners of the mouth that seems to lean toward a smile. A Gray Whale does not have good binocular vision like a human, so she must move her entire body to look at who is near her. Sometimes you can catch a reflection of your own image in a whale's gleaming eye as she looks at you—reflecting back your admiring face.

Playful babies love to splash as they dive under the boat and reappear on the other side for another look. Humans can be equally playful, and downright silly at times, rushing from one side of the boat to the other to watch the whales, splashing the water and often calling out, "Come here babeee…come here mamaaa…you are so beeeautiful." Humans are prone to burst into song, singing everything from "Amazing Grace" to "Baby Beluga" to "Rock Around the Clock." Two Japanese visitors on a *panga* with me sang a traditional Japanese song, "Sakura," which praises the beauty and legacy of the cherry blossoms. The whales seemed mesmerized by the high-pitched, almost hypnotic Japanese melody, hanging around the *panga* for fifteen minutes or more. At one point the whales left, but returned about five minutes later as the singing continued. Inevitably the more time humans spend with the whales, the more likely whale watchers are to resort to a carefree

Visitors from Japan sing in Japanese to a Gray Whale.

ROBIN KOBALY

playfulness and silliness reminiscent of behavior adults usually unleash when in the presence of a human baby. In turn, it seems whales are particularly drawn to *pangas* with children who sing and talk and giggle in high-pitched, playful voices.

When least expected a baby whale can quickly surface and exhale blasts of warm air that mix with a little seawater pooled in the depressions around the two blowholes on the top of his head. Humans caught in this spray are usually startled for a few moments, then laugh, delighted. I believe this is a way they play with us. Often both babies and mothers will open their elongated mouths, exposing their pliable baleen and thick tongues for humans to rub. Sometimes a baby whale fills his mouth with water and then quickly shuts it, splashing those of us leaning over the edge of the boat for closer contact. On occasion mothers roll on their backs and swim belly up to the *pangas,* the most vulnerable and trusting approach a whale can risk. They seem to enjoy having their underside with its long ventral grooves rubbed vigorously.

However, there are also those occasions when a protective mother keeps her newborn from approaching a *panga,* detouring her curious one to what she determines is a safe distance. This seems to happen most often with smaller, younger calves, identifiable by their size, their smooth, barnacle-free skin, and a darker grayish color. In those situations it is a delight just to watch the two swim together, the baby always within the protective shadow of the mother.

I have seen Gray Whales in San Ignacio Lagoon change behavior in recent years. In the early years of my whale watching, the moms and babies would take an interest in our small skiffs floating nearby. At first, a mom would almost always position herself between her baby and the *panga*. Then, if she determined it was safe she would allow her baby to move closer for a visit. Then the mom would roll under the skiff and we would be allowed to stroke her, too. In recent years people have observed some of the moms pushing their young toward our *pangas*. Now mothers sometimes float beneath their babies and gently lift them up so the curious calves can interact longer with the humans.

As exciting as it is to touch the whales, and kiss and hug them, it is also wondrous to watch them swim together, undistracted by nearby human visitors. Their massive bodies glide through the water with great accuracy. Sometimes we sit quietly in the *panga* and watch mothers and babies nearby as they lovingly interact with one another. To witness tenderness and playfulness on such a grand scale with one of the largest animals on earth leaves me speechless. I have seen two-ton baby whales swim onto the huge rounded backs of their moms and playfully roll. Sometimes they do a funny belly flop kind of move on Mom, which she seems to enjoy. Other times the moms lift their babies out of the water and let them splash back down. It reminds me of a human mom lifting her baby up and down overhead and watching the baby giggle. One day I watched two mothers

A Gray Whale's eye clears the water's surface during this "spyhop" in San Ignacio Lagoon.

ROBIN KOBALY

and their calves play side-by-side. The moms floated on their backs as their two-ton babies vigorously splashed and rolled across their mothers' massive bellies.

Other times the whales display vigorous activity, especially if they are mating. In these instances boat drivers are sure to put some distance between the whales and the *pangas* for fear of getting in the way of a massive, fast moving fluke slapping the water. A breaching whale is awe-inspiring. Gray Whales weighing more than twenty tons burst from the water, exposing about three-fourths of their bodies, pivot onto their sides or backs, and then fall back into the water with an explosive splash. It is not unusual for a Gray Whale to breach three or four times in succession, and they have been known to continue for a dozen or more breaches. People have also observed this behavior with calves and juvenile Gray Whales.

It is a common sight to see whales in San Ignacio Lagoon "spyhop" by rising straight up out of the water eight to ten feet, perhaps to take a look around, although nobody knows for sure. Sometimes they turn slowly as if scanning the horizon for thirty seconds or more before slipping underwater once again. At times the whale's eye does not clear the water's surface, a behavior called "heads up." This may indicate the spyhop has nothing to do with looking around. They can spyhop by thrusting their flukes, or if they are in the shallow lagoons they may rest their flukes on the lagoon bottom.

We watch for "footprints" on the lagoon's surface caused by a whale's huge fluke pumping up and down to propel her forward. So much water is displaced by this movement that the pumping creates an upwelling of water, which surfaces as a circular, smooth push of water. Footprints usually indicate a whale is just a few feet below and about to surface.

ROBIN KOBALY

A Gray Whale's dorsal hump and "knuckles"

In the lagoon there are many opportunities to observe whales for extended periods as they make many dives. After several surface dives a Gray will usually make a longer single dive. As a whale slides beneath the water's surface her long serpentine back usually rises above the water, revealing her unique "knuckles" along the dorsal ridge. A Gray Whale does not have a dorsal fin, but about two-thirds of the way down her back is a dorsal hump, followed by six to twelve knuckles along the dorsal ridge that extend to the fluke. As the whale thrusts into a deep dive her fluke will rise straight up. This is a good time to look at the whale's knuckles and fluke, both with unique markings that help identify individual whales. Several minutes later you may get the thrill of watching the whale surface into a spyhop or breach, sometimes quite close to the skiff. I never grow tired of watching this magnificent movement among whales.

The Perfect Morning

One windless morning we set out for whale watching with Ranulfo who drove his *panga, Dolphin II.* The lagoon's glassy surface reflected puffy white clouds. On that particular morning the world seemed to be moving in slow motion. As Ranulfo casually drove out to the whale watching area, we watched mother whales and their babies gracefully slide in and out of the water as if out for a morning stroll. At times the whales would just stop and float, a resting behavior called "logging." Not far from our *panga* we could see loons paddling near the great backs of whales, and beyond that, dolphins popping up every so often.

Osprey passed calmly by overhead, watching for breakfast. A diving tern, as direct and straight as an arrow, zoomed into the water and quickly rose back up with a smelt. Immediately a Western gull chased the tern, trying to steal the meal. The *whoosh* of whales exhaling and inhaling joined with the constant chorus of birds. This is the music of the lagoon.

Ranulfo drove slowly, no rush, scanning the whale watching area for nearby whale activity. He headed toward the mouth of the lagoon with the Pacific Ocean beyond, and stopped. He kept the boat's engine in neutral at a low hum, a sound to which the whales are drawn. Within five minutes whales began approaching our *panga*, interested in a visit. Babies rolled together lazily, playfully. Flukes gently dipped in and out of the calm waters.

At first there were two pair, then three. Whales kept swimming up next to the *panga*, repeatedly, and we massaged their heads and undersides for long periods of time. Ranulfo began counting the whales, all mother and calf pairs, and suddenly declared, "I can't believe this! This is a whale soup." Ten whales floated around us in all directions, taking

Pachico watching visitors greet a friendly whale.

turns approaching the *panga*. We all gave them long gentle strokes as if massaging them. Mothers and babies rubbed heads together, slowly, displaying some of the most tender interactions I have ever witnessed between a mother and baby of *any* species. That morning was dreamlike, filled with a reverence that graced all of us, whales and humans alike.

The Mystery Between Whales and Humans

As whale watchers' days become regulated by morning and afternoon visits to the whales, most of them seem to relax and become more playful themselves. Visitors become enthralled with the wonder and the mystery of interacting with whales in such friendly and trusting encounters. This may also be due in part to the absence of the daily distractions of the technological world with its computers and phones. Many times I have observed visitors let down their guard with one another and begin to delight in one another's company and the extraordinary circumstances of San Ignacio and its inhabitants. Laughter abounds, and sharing stories and secrets and dreams seems to increase with each passing day with the whales. If there are professional photographers or film crews along for the ride, at some point even they will usually put down their equipment, stop being the professional observers, and reach out to touch a friendly whale. I like to think of this place and time with the whales as the "great equalizer." For a short time people's social, economic, cultural, and age differences do not matter. We are all just a group of humans who have come together to meet the whales.

People who visit the lagoon and interact with the whales are usually moved beyond words. One visitor, Wayne, a dairy farmer from Wisconsin and father of eight, took his first vacation in nearly twenty years to accompany his sister to San Ignacio Lagoon. That first morning whale watching, Wayne was excited yet also skeptical about whether or

Ranulfo Mayoral's ink line drawing of Gray Whales

not the whales really do come to the boats for a visit. He thought the claim was almost too good to be true. Within fifteen minutes a mother and calf approached the *panga* and Wayne reached out and touched his first whale. Afterwards, he leaned back, pushed his baseball cap off his forehead and declared, "I can die a happy man now." Somehow, I think he will find his way back to the lagoon and bring a few friends with him.

As much as visitors are enthralled with meeting the whales, it is obvious many of the locals at San Ignacio are continuously awed by the whales. They live here year round and every December greet the returning whales. The locals write songs and stories about the whales, and paint whale pictures on paper, fabric, wood, smooth stones, shells, and T-shirts. Ranulfo Mayoral is an accomplished artist as well as a fisherman and naturalist. He creates detailed, ink line drawings of Gray Whales and babies, reproducing limited editions that he sells to visitors. Other local artists also sell their artwork to visitors who want to take home a reminder of this most unusual experience.

With little prodding, locals tell their stories of exciting or unusual whale encounters with an affection one displays when talking about an old friend. Locals who work as boat drivers and naturalists often take their own families out on the lagoon to visit the whales. One boat driver and naturalist, Pancho Mayoral Aguilar, first took his daughter Sierra out to see the whales when she was eight months old. The following year when the whales returned, she toddled over to her parents with her lifejacket, saying the words "*ballena*" and "whale." She let her parents know in no uncertain terms she was ready to go whale watching again. Perhaps Sierra will follow in the footsteps of her father, and her grandfather, Pachico Mayoral, who was the first to have a friendly interaction with the whales.

While at the whale watching camps there are many opportunities to just sit on the shore, listening and watching for the whales. During the day we can easily see their spouts gushing up to ten feet high, often in watery heart shapes, as they exhale. Frequently whales rise out of the water spyhopping, then slip back into the lagoon as viewers *ooohhhh* and *aaahhh*.

On calm nights we can hear the whales' great blasts of air as they weave back and forth between water and air at a time when the two worlds become seamless. For years I have watched these whale activities in the lagoon from shore and on the *pangas*. I often think about that place on the water's surface where whales and humans meet to share one another's worlds. As much as we humans like to think that we are doing the watching, I am now convinced they are watching us, too.

The whales' trust and vulnerability affect some visitors in profound ways that they have described as life changing. To witness on such a large scale the demonstration of trust, gentleness, and genuine inquisitiveness from another species is a life experience that defies our preconceived ideas of animals and what they are capable of emotionally. These whales display great affection, and intelligence that many humans have never imagined nor experienced—and science cannot yet explain.

Every time we have a friendly encounter I am awed by how much these whales trust us. Many adult whales alive today also were alive in the 1970s and earlier, at a time when whalers hunted them. Now the whales freely approach humans and lift their precious babies for us to touch. Whalers once feared the Gray Whales more than any other because they would kill their hunters in order to defend their own kind. Now, humans are awed by the trust and generosity of spirit these same whales extend to us.

Dick Russell, who has written many books and articles on the Gray Whales and San Ignacio Lagoon, described this feeling most poignantly, "The *pangas* that today propel us among them [the whales] are the same size as those whaleboats. Yet now the grays come beseeching the outstretched hands of people whose forebearers once thrust harpoons....Their forgiveness, indeed their love, is surely one of the planet's profound mysteries."

Photographer Robin Kobaly puts her camera down to greet a whale.

DOUG THOMPSON

Francisco "Pachico" Mayoral

THREE

Keepers of the Lagoon

"This may be as close to heaven as one gets on earth," Pachico Mayoral tells visitors to *Laguna San Ignacio*. Every day Pachico walks out the front door of his home on the lagoon and, depending on the time of year, he can see whales, dolphins, sea turtles, and an array of birds who also consider *Laguna San Ignacio* home. Pachico and his extended family of about twelve live in a village called *La Laguna* on the northeastern shore of the lagoon, the site of the lagoon's oldest fish camp. Five of his six grown children work with him in his whale watching business, Pachico's Eco Tours, the first on the shores of San Ignacio.

Pachico, his family, and other local residents make this lagoon a special place. Those who work with the whales have a great respect and love for the *ballena gris* (Gray Whale). I refer to the local villagers as the keepers of the lagoon because of their respect for and commitment to the whales and the environment. The whales have made it possible for the locals to establish successful, low impact, ecotourism that helps the residents along the shores of the lagoon make a decent living in a difficult environment. The locals understand how important it is to protect the lagoon so the whales will continue to return home each year. They realize the whales are at the heart of ecotourism at San Ignacio Lagoon.

The People of San Ignacio Lagoon

Long before the first humans arrived on the shores of San Ignacio, whales had already been using this birthing lagoon for thousands of years. The landscape looks much the same as it did thousands of years ago after the last Ice Age, when the whales and other indigenous wildlife were the only residents. The area surrounding the lagoon has always been sparse with human inhabitants primarily because there is no outlet for fresh water.

The original people in the area were the Cochimí Indians, who lived by fishing, hunting, and gathering fruits and seeds. Archaeologists have found many spectacular cave paintings and petroglyphs painted several centuries before the first Spanish explorers arrived in 1534. The cave paintings located in the nearby mountains of *Sierra de San Francisco* and *Santa Marta* are considered among the most significant archaeological finds in the world. This cave art suggests that at one time there was an advanced civilization that had created cave art throughout the Baja peninsula.

Museum reproduction of original cave paintings

MURAL, SAN IGNACIO

Located about thirty-five miles to the northeast of San Ignacio Lagoon, the town of San Ignacio is built on the site of an earlier Cochimí settlement centered around an oasis, *Kadakaamán* (Creek of Reeds). An underground stream made this a fertile oasis in the midst of a desert landscape. The Cochimí lived in this area for generations before the first known explorers set foot in the Baja region. The Spanish introduced diseases that wiped out most of the original populations of Baja. Then the Spanish Jesuit missionaries arrived in San Ignacio in 1716 and established one of several missions on the Baja peninsula. The foreigners also brought more diseases that basically decimated the remaining native population. By about the nineteenth century most of the indigenous people of Baja were gone. Today, most of the people in the area are descendants of people who migrated from mainland Mexico.

In the 1920s, the Mexican government established fish camps in the area of San Ignacio Lagoon to increase the fishing population. The entrance to the lagoon was rich in sea turtles, shark, and shrimp, while interior lagoon waters yielded a variety of fish and shellfish, including lobster, bay and fan scallops, *corvina*, sea bass, and halibut.

A few families have lived near the shores of San Ignacio Lagoon for a couple of generations. Some are more recent descendants of ranchers who migrated to this remote lagoon looking for new opportunities. Today, fishing is the primary livelihood for people living at the lagoon. During the busy fishing season, buyers from Ensenada, about five hundred miles to the north, arrive at the lagoon daily. Their trucks are stocked with ice to truck the fresh seafood and fish back to Ensenada.

Several fishing cooperatives catch an array of fish, including halibut and *corvina*. Locals mostly fish using a hand line with multiple hooks or short gillnets on one-day sets. They also dive for clams and scallops, and set traps for lobster and blue crabs. In the ocean the fishers use a variety of methods, including fish traps for *blanco* or *pierna*, and nets and hand lines for bass, yellow tail, and *corvina*. Depending on what species of fish they are after, some fishers travel more than twenty miles into the Pacific Ocean to set up their fishing gear. It can be dangerous navigating in rough seas with their small *pangas*, which average about twenty-two to twenty-six feet in length. They must pull up their fishing gear by hand with the day's catch. Every couple of years a fisherman dies at sea, usually from trying to navigate between the moody Pacific Ocean and the mouth of *Laguna San Ignacio*.

Welcoming the Whales

In December the locals who live on the shores of the lagoon begin watching for the whales. Pregnant whales are usually the first to arrive, ready to birth their young in the warm, calm waters of the lagoon. Over the years, villagers have identified many returning whales by unique markings on their flukes or bodies, or by their distinct "knuckles" along the dorsal ridge. They have named some of the familiar whales; *Cara Blanca* (white head), *Cortada* (cuts on head), *Mancha Rosa* (pink spots), and a very friendly whale, *Valentina*—"the whale who hugs *pangas*." One unique whale who has been coming to the lagoon for about twelve years is *Sin Cola*—"the whale with no tail." Naturalists speculate she probably lost her tail because fishing line wrapped around the base of the tail and gradually cut it off. Scientists have spotted *Sin Cola* traveling on the regular migration route. She swims by moving her tail stem sideways while she is on her side.

In my many years of visiting the lagoon, whale-watching visitors have also nicknamed familiar whales: Patches (distinct white patches on her head), White Scar (a sizable scar on his back), Chunky (a big chunk of flesh missing from her tail), and Grace (graceful movements).

For the past eight years, boat driver and naturalist Ranulfo Mayoral has seen one particular whale during several whale seasons. He named her Trini (short for Trinidad) and could easily identify her because of three parallel white marks on her right side and her distinct, evenly spaced knuckles. In 2006 I was in a *panga* with Ranulfo when he spotted Trini. Usually calm and steady, Ranulfo jumped with glee at the sight of Trini whom he had not seen for a couple of years. He moved his boat closer to Trini and greeted her with great joy as she approached with her new calf. Ranulfo gave her some exuberant strokes on the head and admired her baby. Later that same day, Ranulfo proudly showed me a photograph of Trini he took several years ago when she was in the lagoon. He keeps Trini's photo in a worn family photo album that also includes many family pictures of his wife and children. For the rest of the day Ranulfo had a big smile, delighted to meet up with his old friend Trini.

Photo of Trini that Ranulfo keeps in his family photo album.

RANULFO MAYORAL

Pachico Mayoral's Legacy

Francisco "Pachico" Mayoral was the first in Laguna San Ignacio to have friendly interactions with the Gray Whales. It was a turning point for the lagoon locals as well as for the whales. Most of the residents consider Pachico to be the honorary supervisor of the lagoon and he participates in all the important discussions regarding fishing, whale watching, and community activities. Pachico, who turned 66 in 2006, is highly respected among the locals as "a man who thinks before he acts" and who studies problems before he speaks. He has an air of quiet authority yet at the same time imparts friendliness, greeting visitors with a wide smile, and a firm handshake. Anyone who knows Pachico, or has the opportunity to talk with him for a while knows he truly loves the whales and the lagoon. "The whales are family to me," he says in Spanish, his sparkling dark eyes as intense as the whales' eyes.

Pachico's wife, Carmen Aguilar, has lived on the shores of the lagoon her entire life. She is respected for her knowledge of native plants for medicinal remedies, and many locals turn to her for advice on healing plants and herbs to treat their aliments. Carmen's family roots at the lagoon date back to about the 1870s, and her grandfather is considered one of the founders of the small fishing village, *La Laguna*. As a young man Pachico traveled to the lagoon to fish. When he was about twenty years old he met Carmen and decided to move to the lagoon. Pachico and Carmen soon married and they raised their six children along the shores of *Laguna San Ignacio*.

For many years El Vizcaíno Biosphere Reserve administration has asked Pachico to oversee San Ignacio Lagoon's two small islands, *Isla Garzas* (Heron Island) and *Isla Pelicanos* (Pelican Island), in clear view from his front door. The islands are located in the upper, northeastern part of the lagoon, about a fifteen-minute boat ride from Pachico's home.

These two islands are known for the thousands of nesting birds, especially Brandt's cormorants, double-breasted cormorants, osprey, American oystercatchers, egrets, herons, gulls, and peregrine falcons. The islands are off limits to the general public because they are considered "core zones" of the Biosphere Reserve. Pachico makes sure all visitors to the islands have official permits, and he usually escorts them to the islands. During nesting season no one can land on the islands because disturbing the breeding birds from their nests can result in devastating egg predation by gulls.

Ranulfo Mayoral and his family live next door to his parents, Pachico and Carmen, in *La Laguna*. In many ways Ranulfo has followed in his father's footsteps—especially in his love of the lagoon and the whales. When Ranulfo was eight years old his dad took him to see the whales. "I was scared," recalls Ranulfo. "We were following one whale in the boat and another whale was following us. We turned to look and the whale behind us was about two feet from our boat. I saw the fluke and I jumped to the other side of the boat." In 1979 when Ranulfo was only seventeen years old, he began working on whale watching tours with Pachico.

Today, marine biologists, naturalists, researchers, film crews, and still photographers seek out Pachico and

Ranulfo Mayoral driving his panga during whale watching season.

ROBIN KOBALY

Ranulfo. Both are known for their understanding of whale behavior and the lagoon wildlife. Ranulfo's specialty is working with film crews to get the best natural lighting for photographing and filming whales. He is also a bird expert and has personally identified 181 of the approximately 200 bird species at San Ignacio Lagoon. Ranulfo keeps year-round data on his bird observations and is a great resource for bird watchers.

Ranulfo has a quiet, steady presence and an immediate smile and friendly handshake for visitors, much like his father. Often in the evenings at the whale watching camp, while others regale one another with stories of the day, Ranulfo sits quietly creating intricate, black-ink line drawings of whales. He also updates his turtle log. Ranulfo tracks turtles in the lagoon on behalf of *Grupo Tortuguero de las Californias*, a nonprofit conservation group in *La Paz, Baja California Sur*. The organization hired Ranulfo and another fisherman and whale watching guide, Paco Ficher, to monitor endangered turtles. Paco is the son of Maldo Ficher, who co-owns one of the whale watching camps involved in turtle research and rehabilitation. In particular, Ranulfo and Paco track great green sea turtles and loggerhead turtles who feed on red crab in the lagoon. Prior to the 1980s green sea turtle was a favorite meal for the locals. Today, hunting a turtle could lead to thousands of dollars in fines and jail time.

Ranulfo Mayoral

ROBIN KOBALY

Ranulfo and Paco are paid year-round to gather vital information on the turtles' habits and behavior. Ranulfo keeps a meticulous journal of all turtles tracked, using a fine, black-ink pen for most of his entries and notes. When tracking a turtle they note the turtle's I.D. number, tag number, personal name, and yearly dates when the turtle was sighted. They also note the type of net the turtle was caught in—cotton or nylon; the depth of the net; depth of the water; visibility in the water; and ocean conditions, among other details before releasing the turtle back into the lagoon. Ranulfo takes great pride in his ongoing turtle log, and gives affectionate and sometimes fun names to the turtles he tracks. There is *Chago,* Nora, Lucy, *Valentina,* Socrates, *Sierrita* (in honor of his little niece), *Blanca,* Mickey Mouse, and Frankenstein, who has an odd number and arrangement of scutes, the bony plates on the turtle's shell.

There is no doubt Ranulfo and Pachico are dedicated to this lagoon—the whales, the birds, the fish, and the landscape. They are the experts, the ones who stand on its shores daily, fish its depths, and observe countless activities from their boats. Browned and chiseled by a life on the sea, father and son have a quiet dignity and a gentle gregariousness. Perhaps their years with the whales keep them happy.

Future Generations at the Lagoon

Pachico has eight grandchildren as of 2006, several of whom are learning the ways of the whales and the lagoon. Ranulfo and his wife, Emilia Peralta, have three children; Adilene, Antonio, and Isabella. Ranulfo is teaching his eldest child, Adilene, who turned sixteen in 2006, how to monitor and track sea turtles as well as understand the ways of the whales. A delightful children's book on the Gray Whales of San Ignacio, *Adelina's Whales,* by Richard Sobol (Dutton 2003), features Adilene's unique life on the shores of the lagoon. It also talks about the threat of corporate interests developing a salt factory at San Ignacio. In the book's foreword, written by Robert F. Kennedy, Jr., he wisely observes that Adilene and other children who visit the whales seem to instinctively know "humans don't have the right to destroy what we cannot create." Fortunately, the proposed salt factory was stopped in 2000 due to international protest and efforts by millions of people.

Adilene is a serious student and now travels the thirty-five miles into the town of San Ignacio where she attends high school. During the week she lives in a dormitory provided by the Mexican government, and comes home on weekends. She is considering a career in *Turismo Alternativo* (Alternative Tourism) offered at the University of Baja California Sur in *La Paz*, about two hundred seventy-five miles to the south of San Ignacio. The family will welcome Adilene's professional skills to complement their ecotourism business. With encouragement from her parents and grandparents, Adilene is becoming a future keeper of the lagoon, along with her cousins and other young people living at the lagoon.

Guadalupe "Lupita" Murillo grew up on the shores of the lagoon in a community of about fifty people, mostly family, called *La Base*. When Lupita was about six years old, one of her uncles, a boat driver, took her family to see the whales. "I was so happy to be there, touching the whales," recalls Lupita, who turned twenty-one in 2006. "We would go out to see the whales every season." When Lupita was about eleven years old she began fishing with her grandpa. "I fished with my *abuelo*. I called him *'Tata'* sometimes. We fished together for eight years and we were the only boat fishing with a single hand line. We got friendly whales near our boat, but my *abuelo* would move. I wanted to touch the whales but my grandpa moved the boat away because he wanted to fish." Lupita describes her grandpa as a wonderful man who taught her many things about the lagoon and the fish. He died in 2005 and Lupita thinks of him every day, especially when she is on the lagoon. "My grandpa didn't know it, but he was really an ecological person. When we went to fish, we could've caught hundreds of fish, but we only fished for what we needed. He would tell me, 'There will be more fish tomorrow.'"

In 2002 Lupita applied to participate in a special conservation program, Nature Guide Training, offered by a nonprofit organization, Rare, which supports local ecotourism efforts. Lupita wanted to follow in the footsteps of her uncles and male cousins and work with whale watching at the lagoon. Her grandpa supported her decision and encouraged her to take the biggest step of her life. She was only seventeen years old and nervous, but she longed to learn more about conservation and working with the whales. Eighty students tested and only twenty were accepted, including Lupita. After graduation Lupita was hired by one of the whale watching camps because she was an excellent student. She became the first female guide at San Ignacio Lagoon. "The job is amazing and I meet a lot of really fun and different people from all over the world," explains Lupita, who loves to laugh heartily and often. But she adds on a serious note, "People who don't like women guides, that's the hardest. Some local people say to me I should get married and have kids."

Lupita Murillo is the first trained female guide and naturalist at San Ignacio Lagoon.

ROBIN KOBALY

Lupita's grandfather, Jesus Murillo Aguilar, (right) and her cousin bring in their fish caught with a single hand line.

Lupita works full time as a guide during whale watching season, and in the off season either fishes in the lagoon or leads kayaking trips in *La Paz*. Now bilingual, Lupita continues to broaden her interests and horizons, however, she continues to call San Ignacio Lagoon her home. "I don't want people to come and make big hotels or restaurants at the lagoon. I really worry about that now. To keep the lagoon the way we have it now we must teach the young people to take care of it. We have to place the future care of the lagoon in the hands of our young people today." Lupita's oldest brother, Pedro, turned thirteen in 2006 and now he thinks about getting involved with ecotourism. Lupita is already teaching her six-year-old brother, Gabriel, and his friends how to be respectful of the lagoon. The first lessons in conservation are: "Pick up trash," and, "Do not kill small animals."

When asked what she has learned from the whales, Lupita answers, "We have to learn to forgive the way the whales do. The people who come and touch the whales can imagine what it was like when we used to kill the whales. Yet, the whales have forgiven us. They could kill us easy, but they don't. Instead they come and bring their babies and they are gentle with us." Lupita sits quietly for a few moments, then adds, "I really think about God putting those whales here to teach us humans to forgive—to open our eyes and see."

FOUR

Whale Watching Camps

*T*he first whale watchers of the season arrive at San Ignacio Lagoon as early as the last week of December, just as the whales arrive. This is when many of the lagoon's fishermen put away their gear and turn to their other line of work—ecotourism. San Ignacio Lagoon is one of the best examples internationally of successful ecotourism. Here the local residents work to invigorate their local economy, while at the same time preserving their environment. Community members make the decisions for local commerce that are compatible with regulations established by El Vizcaíno Biosphere Reserve. Local residents and whale watching camps are all involved in efforts to protect the lagoon, working closely with Mexican and international environmental groups. (Chapter Five details the Biosphere Reserve protections and government regulations.)

Visitors stay at one of the six whale watching camps permitted at the lagoon. Local residents own four of the camps: Pachico's Eco Tours, Baja Ecotours, *Ecoturismo Kuyimá,* and Antonio's Ecotours. Individuals outside of San Ignacio Lagoon operate two additional camps, Baja Discovery and Baja Expeditions. All six camps employ many of the lagoon's residents as well as workers from other areas of Baja. During whale watching season this means employment for nearly one hundred locals who work in a variety of jobs, including boat drivers, certified trained naturalists, cooks, and support personnel for the camps.

Boat permits are required during whale watching season in the lagoon and issued on a limited basis to lagoon residents. This means the locals oversee the whale watching at San Ignacio, and the local fishermen use their *pangas* for whale watching outings. As of 2006, San Ignacio Lagoon whale watching regulations allow no more than sixteen

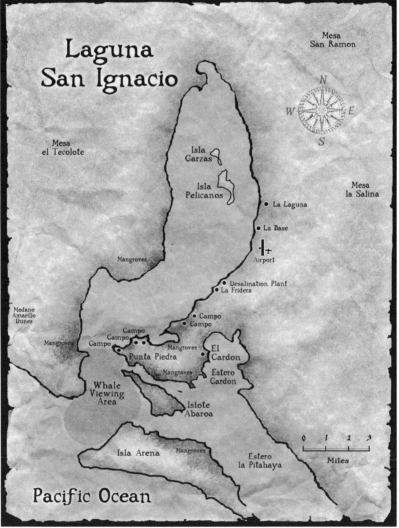

pangas in the designated whale watching area at any given time in order to not harass the whales. A total of twenty-nine boat permits are issued to locals for whale watching. In addition, the regulations allow no more than two long-range whale watching vessels in the lagoon at any time. These larger vessels must also use local boat drivers and their *pangas* while in the designated whale watching area.

Each year the boat drivers elect one driver who sits in the "rescue" boat at Rocky Point *(Punta Piedra)* at the entrance to the whale watching area. Everyone must check in with him when entering and leaving the whale watching area. This boat driver is in charge of tracking the number of boats going in and out of the lagoon, mindful the regulations are followed by everyone. *Laguna San Ignacio* is a great example of the local community regulating itself and cooperatively working together for the best outcome for ecotourism and for the protection of the whales.

Most of the fishers who drive their twenty-one foot *pangas* on daily whale watching excursions enjoy their months of hosting international visitors and getting to know people beyond their villages, country, and culture. During whale season the boat drivers are busy every day. In addition to whale watching tours they must keep up with daily maintenance of their *pangas.* Everything is done manually at the lagoon because there are no fuel or maintenance docks, marine hardware stores, or auto parts stores. The drivers must siphon gasoline from fifty-gallon drums in the back of their trucks, and carry five-gallon containers to their boats on the shore. At very low tide, the walk can be several hundred yards each way. The fishers of San Ignacio Lagoon are masters of invention and recycling, and are some of the best mechanics you will ever meet. The old car or truck sitting along side a house can look like useless junk to an outsider, but to the locals these automotive carcasses serve as "parts stores" for their current vehicles and boats. It is a constant challenge to

Valentín Liera Aguilar oversees the whale-watching area from Rocky Point.

keep the boats and cars running in this dusty, salty environment, far from the conveniences of city life.

Local Residents Train for Ecotourism

Every year the local boat drivers and naturalists give tours to several thousand people traveling from around the world to see the Gray Whales at San Ignacio Lagoon. They must have considerable knowledge of the lagoon and whale behavior in order to answer the numerous questions whale watchers ask. They also must maneuver around the whales without harassing them, yet also make it possible for visitors to see and hopefully touch the whales.

Many boat drivers and local naturalists received their training from "Rare," a small nonprofit organization based in the United States that started its global work in the early 1970s. Rare's Nature Guide Training Program provides natural history classes, basic marketing skills for ecotourism, conversational English classes, technical support, first aid training, and resources so residents can maintain and protect their own environment while at the same time making a successful living from ecotourism. For communities in environmentally sensitive places, Rare helps residents create alternatives to high impact fishing, logging, and other environmentally harmful activities.

In 1995 Rare began training residents of San Ignacio Lagoon for work in ecotourism, offering the Guide Training Program. As of 2006 Rare has trained about eighteen residents of San Ignacio Lagoon, providing tremendous opportunities for advancement in ecotourism. A good example of Rare's success at San Ignacio Lagoon is Pancho Mayoral Aguilar, Pachico's son and Ranulfo's younger brother. When Pancho was fourteen years old, he caught endangered turtles and sold them at what he describes as "a very good price." However, when Pancho graduated from Rare's training program in 1995-1996, he learned the value of protecting the environment and its natural resources. Today he is a well-paid naturalist guide, and runs whale watching tours and kayak trips in Baja. He also works as an environmental educator with the National Outdoor Leadership School (NOLS), teaching young people from the U.S. and Mexico about the region's natural resources.

Rare's success working with San Ignacio Lagoon residents is amplified worldwide with similar successes in communities looking for ways to preserve their natural resources while making a living. Rare supports hundreds of grassroots conservationists in the Pacific, Latin America, Africa, and Asia. The organization's mission is to turn "average citizens into life-long advocates for the environment by helping them better their lives through more sustainable livelihoods." This has certainly worked for residents of San Ignacio Lagoon.

The Camps

The ride from the dirt airstrip by San Ignacio Lagoon to the whale watching camps on the southern shore can take from fifteen minutes to an hour, depending on camp location and weather. The closer the camp is to the mouth of the lagoon, the longer the drive, but the shorter the boat ride to watching the whales. However, the shorter the drive to a camp then the longer the boat ride to reach the designated whale watching area.

Washboard road conditions and mounds of sand that expand and contract with the rain, wind, and sun make the dirt road to camp an adventure in itself. The roads around the lagoon, many across salt flats, give new meaning to the word bumpy. Several camps use vans to bring people from the small town of San Ignacio, a rough ride that can take two hours or more, depending on weather conditions. Yet, despite the inconvenience of this difficult dirt road, it is this same rough road that keeps the lagoon off the beaten path and insulated from much of the outside world. You have to really *want* to see the whales, and your vehicle has to be up for the challenge in order to make the trek from San Ignacio town to the lagoon!

ROBIN KOBALY

Locals and guests play volleyball on the edge of the lagoon.

Although the lagoon is isolated, visitors are usually surprised at the comfort provided in these simple whale-watching camps—a reflection of the ingenuity of the residents working with limited resources. Most of the camps use either a collection of large white canvas tents or small *cabañas* that usually house two visitors comfortably. Most camps have a general meeting and eating area in a larger *palapa,* (a round room with windows and a roof of palm fronds) or a mess tent. There are also solar showers and simple ecological latrines. Wind generators and solar panels with marine, deep-storage batteries are commonly used to supply a camp's simple electrical needs. The locals also use wind generators and solar panels for electricity in their homes. At the end of whale watching season, camps run by nonresidents are completely dismantled. Locally owned camps have simple structures that remain standing year-round and serve other purposes, including a kids' summer camp and overnight accommodations for visitors stopping by at other times of the year. These structures also provide a place for fishers to camp for a night if needed.

For visitors wanting a hot shower, all of the camps offer solar heated water. The sun heats enough water by late afternoon for people to enjoy a short, but satisfying shower. Local residents of the lagoon often note the cultural differences, amused at how tourists, especially from the United States, expect to find hot water everywhere. The locals find hot water showers a little uncomfortable because they are used to the ambient temperature of water for their showers.

At San Ignacio Lagoon, much like most of Baja, there is no running water and no power other than what the locals can generate. In addition, there is no post office or mail delivery, no newspaper, no gas stations, and limited phone service at nearby community stores. Until last year, there was no fresh water source within twenty miles of the lagoon. Around 2002 local residents began to have access to more efficient environmental technologies such as solar power and wind generators. In 2004 the community built a small desalination plant to supply residents with fresh water. The plant is located within five miles of most lagoon residents' homes. Before then, the locals had to drive as far as thirty miles to truck in heavy fifty-gallon containers of water. In 2006 a cell phone tower was built on a hill in the town of San Ignacio thirty-five miles away. Depending on how the wind is blowing across the flat landscape, residents at the lagoon can get occasional cell phone service. It seems the best reception occurs when the air is still. Lagoon residents now have a land phone at a small store in the nearby town of *El Centro* that is reliable although expensive. Another five miles to the southwest in the fishing cooperative of *El Cardon* there is another land phone, also expensive but reliable. The local school in *El Centro* provides Internet service for lagoon residents for a few hours in the afternoon. Some locals have email addresses, and most whale watching camps have websites providing extensive information on their services, costs, and the whales. All of these modern additions make life far easier for the residents of San Ignacio Lagoon.

If lagoon residents have medical needs they first travel to San Ignacio town. If further tests are needed, or if local doctors cannot manage the medical situation because they lack the equipment, locals drive about two hours to *Santa Rosalia,* located on the eastern shore of the Baja Peninsula on the Sea of Cortez. When I asked a local what he does in a medical emergency, he replied, "Don't have one." For the whale watching camps, there is a traveling doctor who visits the camps upon request.

One of the whale watching camps situated on the lagoon.

ROBIN KOBALY

The First Whale Watching Camps

About a year after Pachico Mayoral's first encounter with a friendly whale, he established San Ignacio's first whale watching camp on the shoreline near his home. In those early years few people would brave the rugged, bone-jarring dirt road from the town of San Ignacio out to the lagoon. A hardy traveler could drive this dirt road at about fifteen miles an hour on a good, dry day. If it rained, all bets were off. The early Baja tourists of the 1960s and 1970s needed four-wheel drive vehicles along with extra water, gasoline, and an adventurous spirit.

In December 1973 workers completed the final mile of Mexico Highway 1, officially called *Carretera Peninsular Benito Juárez*. This 1,060-mile paved highway, mostly one lane in each direction, is considered the lifeline of the Baja California Peninsula. It runs the length of Baja California from the northern border with the United States to *Cabo San Lucas* at the tip of southern Baja. After the completion of Mexico Highway 1, tourists slowly began venturing into Baja to explore, more confident they could make the trip to San Ignacio and points beyond. Before then, only experienced Baja travelers ventured down the peninsula exploring virtually untouched landscapes—a time that they now fondly refer to as "the good ol' days."

There were few land-based whale-watching camps aside from Pachico's in those first years, although an occasional whale-watching tour boat would travel from San Diego to San Ignacio to see the whales. After Pachico Mayoral established his whale watching camp at San Ignacio, it was more than fifteen years before three other Mexican-owned camps were established. The 1970s and 1980s were a transitional time for San Ignacio Lagoon as Mexico began efforts to protect all of the Baja birthing lagoons. A 1979 decree from the Mexican government had designated *Laguna San Ignacio* as a whale refuge. In

The challenging dirt road leads from San Ignacio town to the lagoon.

1988 El Vizcaíno Biosphere Reserve was created, and local residents began to organize to establish a more extensive ecotourism business.

In the 1980s local fishermen organized and lobbied the Mexican government to get the permits to be the designated boat drivers for whale watching in San Ignacio Lagoon. They knew local ecotourism was a vital part of maintaining a livelihood at the lagoon and they did not want outsiders taking work away from the local residents. In 1988 regulations were established to make locals the designated *panga* drivers. This ecotourism work provides another source of income for the locals, who depended primarily on fishing.

Since then local fishers have been the official escorts for whale watching in the lagoon, using their own *pangas* that comfortably seat seven or eight people. Most of the drivers know the lagoon inside and out because it is an integral part of their fishing grounds. They respect the regulations Biosphere Reserve naturalists established to keep human visitors from disturbing the mating and birthing whales. These boat drivers take great pride in self-regulation and working together in order to protect the whales and the environment while at the same time being grateful for the additional income.

The Early Days of Whale Watching Camps

A year or so after Pachico began land-based whale watching tours an outsider visited the lagoon and established a whale watching camp. Piet Van de Mark, one of Baja's early adventurers from the states, became a pioneer in ecotours with his fledgling company, Baja Frontier Tours. Piet began whale watching at *Ojo de Liebre* in 1967. He first visited *Laguna San Ignacio* in 1973 and recalls that in those early days "there were no other outsiders at the lagoon other than an occasional boat down from San Diego." Eventually Piet established two camps at San Ignacio Lagoon—one that people could drive to, and the other at Rocky Point (*Punta Piedra*) on the lagoon, which could only be reached by a small boat.

Local camp owner, Antonio Aguilar (left) and his friend entertaining guests after dinner.

ROBIN KOBALY

In 1975 another outsider enamored with the lagoon, Mike Symons, founded an ecotourism business called Wilderness Expeditions, and that same year set up his first whale watching camp. He ran trips to San Ignacio Lagoon for the San Diego Natural History Museum and other Southern California groups. Mike would take people down in four-wheel-drive Chevy Suburbans, or fly them into the area in small airplanes. Mike was also the first at the lagoon to experiment with a portable solar panel as a source of power. The local lagoon residents had no source of electricity or power at that time with the possible exception of a couple of noisy old generators. Most lagoon residents relied on kerosene and candles. Mike ended his whale watching trips to San Ignacio in 1982 because "it was too much work and no one was making any money." However, he still visits Pachico and his family, and of course, the whales, almost every year. After the 1988 whale watching season,

Piet also stopped sponsoring trips to San Ignacio and moved his whale watching expeditions back to *Ojo de Liebre*. Not long after that, other whale watching camps developed at San Ignacio Lagoon.

A Lifetime of Leading Whale Expeditions

My introduction to Baja and the whales came from my biology professor, Dennis L. Bostic, who taught at Palomar College in San Marcos, California. A well-known professor with a colorful personality, he had a great enthusiasm for his students, and for introducing them to the world of natural history. In particular, Dennis loved Baja—both the people and the landscape. Dennis was one of those hardy pioneers of environmentalism who explored Baja for years, taking his students with him. In 1972 he founded Biological Educational Expeditions to educate students while traveling with them to Baja's remote and fascinating landscapes. I was one of his students and I joined him on the Baja trips with a caravan of four jeeps loaded with supplies. We traveled and explored for weeks at a time. This was before Highway 1 had been completed, so we hauled extra gas and as much water as possible because these essential commodities were in short supply in Baja's backcountry.

In the early 1970s Dennis created a study-cruise to explore the offshore islands of Baja and the hidden lagoons along the Pacific Coast. I was lucky enough to be on one of the first trips in February 1974. We left from San Diego and traveled as far south as *Ojo de Liebre* to see the Gray Whales. This was the first time I had seen these magnificent creatures up close since my first encounter with a Gray Whale as a teenage surfer in the waters off Huntington Beach, California.

The numerous trips to Baja inspired Dennis to co-write an anthology with other early advocates for Baja's Gray Whales. Writers for this anthology included Brian Cooper, Peter Ott, Janet Sprague, Frank

Rokop, and Steve Leatherwood with editorial assistance from Margie Stinson. His book, *A Natural History Guide to the Pacific Coast and North Central Baja California*, was first published in 1975. Sadly, Dennis died in an auto accident the same year his book was published. Today, when you mention Dennis to the longtime locals of *Laguna San Ignacio* they will tell you, "He was a man who was drawn to the wonder of Baja, and one who had respect for the way of life here." It was Dennis's enthusiasm and love of nature that first inspired me years ago, and still inspires me today with the annual expeditions I lead to San Ignacio.

On my first expedition to San Ignacio, I led about thirty adventurous whale watchers. We sailed on *The Searcher*, a ninety-five-foot long-range vessel. It was a seven-day trip departing from San Diego, allowing for two days traveling down, three days at the lagoon, and two days to return. We stopped at *Isla San Benitos* on the way, about 320 miles south of San Diego. On the return trip we stopped and explored *Isla Cedros*, about two hundred miles north of San Ignacio Lagoon.

That first trip was a rough ride on the open seas, especially the return to San Diego. The Pacific Ocean was anything but calm. We had several incredible interactions with a couple of friendly Gray Whales at the lagoon. That experience profoundly affected me, and has kept me returning to this lagoon almost every year since. At that time I did not know about the locals' friendly encounters with Gray Whales. Unfortunately, in the early days those of us visiting the lagoon on long-range tour boats did not have much interaction with the local residents. I would later learn they had a lot to teach me about the whales, the lagoon, and their invaluable role in preserving the lagoon and surrounding landscape.

Over the years taking groups of whale watchers to San Ignacio, I met several biologists and researchers who studied the Gray Whales. Among them were marine biologists Mary Lou Jones and Steven Swartz; Bruce

Artwork created by Teresa de Varela, an artist with
Mar Azul *in San Ignacio Lagoon.*

Mate, who developed a satellite tagging system; Jim Darling; Jim Sumich; Mike Bursk; and Marilyn Dalheim, among others. In those early days, before there were comfortable whale watching camps, the arrival of our long-range boats in the lagoon was always a welcome sight for the researchers. They spent many a week in tents with the wind and sand. In exchange for a talk on the Gray Whales, we offered the researchers warm showers, great food, beer, and wine. After the shower, the researchers would visit with our guests while we all shared a meal. These researchers knew the boat would be back down in a certain time period, so we would take their mail back to San Diego. And on the return trip we brought them needed supplies, and in general made life a little easier.

All the people I mention have gone on to shape their work and lives around the ocean and sea life. Many have become well-known scientists, teachers, writers, and filmmakers. What we have shared is the wonder of Gray Whales, who changed their behavior in our life time—from aggressive to friendly—and we were all early witnesses to that remarkable shift.

As I became more involved with the whales and with leading whale watching trips, I started offering educational presentations and outdoor natural-history experiences. I lectured at local colleges, high schools, health clubs, and a variety of other venues, driven to let the general public know about the magnificent Gray Whales. I would talk and show slides and 16 mm film footage I had taken of the friendly whales at San Ignacio Lagoon. It had only been in 1971 that the United States had hunted its last whale, and the idea of watching the whales instead of killing them was really taking hold with people. I was committed to "spreading the word" like some kind of whale evangelist.

Mexico took a crucial step for conservation and the Gray Whales when it formed El Vizcaíno Biosphere Reserve in 1988, which includes San Ignacio Lagoon. As a result, whale watching in the lagoon became far more restrictive in order to protect the

Sextos and Teresa de Varela of "Gitanos."
Teresa also works with local artists.

whales. This was good because it also got visitors to interact more with the local fishermen and use their *pangas*. This was the beginning of true ecotourism with land-based camps—and the locals were in charge.

I continued the annual trips to San Ignacio by boat until the early 1990s when I decided to lead whale watching tours with base camps at the lagoon. These turned into five-day trips arriving by plane. This allowed for more time with the whales because flying eliminated four days of boat travel.

In December 2000 I co-founded The SummerTree Institute, a nonprofit organization, along with Robin Kobaly, my wife, who is a botanist, wildlife biologist, and photographer. The SummerTree Institute focuses on environmental education and expeditions that are designed to make environmental education interesting. In 2005 we expanded our scope by adding *Instituto SummerTree* based in Ensenada, Mexico. We work with marine biologist José Ángel Sánchez Pacheco, who was closely involved with establishing Mexico's El Vizcaíno

ROBIN KOBALY

*Pachico Mayoral and
José Ángel Sánchez Pacheco*

Biosphere Reserve. In particular, José was responsible for the studies to determine safe levels of boats for whale watching and to define specific whale watching areas in the Baja birthing lagoons. His findings established the number of *pangas* allowed in San Ignacio Lagoon at any one time, and designated the area for whale watching that does not interfere with the whales' mating and birthing.

Instituto SummerTree is working with the local community to establish a community art center in the local village, *El Centro*, located about one mile from the lagoon. Members of this local art cooperative, *Mar Azul*, have begun to sell their artwork to tourists visiting San Ignacio Lagoon. Teresa de Varela, an artist and musician, helped launch *Mar Azul* with help from lagoon residents. Other endeavors sponsored by *Instituto SummerTree* include expanding the lagoon's ecotourism season with bird watching and sea turtle ecotours. We also are developing educational programs for rural villages that will be delivered in a traveling educational bus. If the residents of *Laguna San Ignacio* and the surrounding area of *Baja Sur* know the value of their natural resources, they will be actively involved in sustainable conservation.

FIVE

Protecting
the Lagoon

T hose who are fortunate to visit San Ignacio Lagoon are always in awe of the stark, yet breathtaking landscape. Add to this the incredible experience of interacting with friendly Gray Whales in the wild and most people express disbelief that such a place exists. Most agree that interacting with Gray Whales is unlike anything they have ever experienced. Some call it transformational, and for others it is spiritual. At the very least a whale watching trip to San Ignacio Lagoon is a unique experience that is hard to compare with any other life experience—and certainly unforgettable. Even the cynical, worldly visitor who sees these magnificent whales in this sparkling blue lagoon leaves with a new-found respect for the whales' right to share the oceans and to have protected environments worldwide.

Over the years Mexico has taken a series of actions to protect the Gray Whales' birthing lagoons along Baja's west coast. In many ways the Gray Whale has become a symbol of Mexico's commitment to environmental protection. The Mexican government as well as local residents working with environmentalists in Mexico and the United States have made significant progress to protect San Ignacio Lagoon. Yet despite these efforts there have been serious threats in recent times that could one day harm the lagoon and the surrounding environment.

ROBIN KOBALY

San Ignacio Lagoon

When newcomers visit the whales, most want to be reassured that San Ignacio Lagoon is protected and the whales will be safe and unfettered by human progress. As of 2006, most of the southern shore of the lagoon is protected, but this is an ongoing, complex process. Hand-in-hand with protecting the area is the need to protect the livelihood of hundreds of people who live along its shores. If the locals cannot make a living, they cannot stay to conserve the environment.

In recent years people have argued about the benefits and the drawbacks of more whale watchers visiting the Baja birthing lagoons. A handful of early visitors to Baja fondly remember the birthing lagoons in the 1960s and 1970s before there were many whale watchers. Since then, *Ojo de Liebre, Guerrero Negro,* and *Bahia Magdalena* have all been impacted by business development, including salt mines that started in the 1950s, which led to subsequent port traffic. Fortunately, *Laguna*

San Ignacio has been spared development by outside interests, in large part because residents have been working with environmental groups to preserve the area.

On the one hand, whale watching in the lagoons definitely attracts attention from developers who may want to exploit the environment. Yet it is because people from many international communities now know about San Ignacio Lagoon and its importance to the Gray Whales that this lagoon may ultimately be spared the fallout of commercialism. *Laguna San Ignacio* has also become a unique success story in ecotourism, which may be its saving grace. Many local residents have benefited financially from whale watching in their lagoon while at the same time protecting the Gray Whales. And the overhead for whale upkeep is low. The whales only need a safe lagoon to return to each year, and they will keep coming back! In turn, the whales' yearly return to home waters makes it possible for local residents to make a living with ecotourism and continue their vital role as the keepers of the lagoon.

First Efforts to Protect San Ignacio Lagoon

Mexico has been on the cutting edge of whale protection since the mid-1930s when Mexico decided to stop allowing whaling in Mexican waters. Mexico also participated in the first international efforts to protect several species of whales from extinction. Before then Mexico allowed extensive whaling off both coasts of the Baja peninsula. In 1933 Mexico recognized the Geneva Convention for the Protection of Whales, and in 1938 signed the "Convention for the Regulation of Whaling" sponsored by the League of Nations. Written in 1931, this document was the first effort to protect some whale species in response to international public outcry at the wholesale slaughter of whales worldwide. Some estimates claim that by the 1930s there were less than one thousand Eastern

Pacific Gray Whales left due to whale hunting. In 1949 Mexico became a member of the International Whaling Commission (IWC), and remains to this day opposed to the resumption of whaling.

Carl Leavitt Hubbs, a Professor of Biology at the Scripps Institution of Oceanography, University of California, San Diego, took pioneering steps to conduct Gray Whale research in the winter of 1944 at a time when no one in the scientific community or in the general public had any interest in Gray Whales. Most people thought the Pacific coast Gray Whale migration had ceased since the population had been hunted to near extinction. Just a month after arriving at Scripps Institution, Professor Hubbs began monitoring Gray Whales at a rooftop lookout on Ritter Hall at Scripps. With help from graduate students and a pair of binoculars, Hubbs counted Gray Whales, plotted their positions and speed, and noted their behavior.

Carl Hubbs worked closely with his wife, Laura Clark Hubbs, who had a Masters degree in mathematics. Although Laura Hubbs was never on the payroll at Scripps, it was generally acknowledged that she worked and traveled side-by-side with her husband, conducting research. Carl Hubbs made the first aerial assessment of gray whales in San Ignacio Lagoon in 1948. Interestingly, Hubbs enlisted the famed actor Errol Flynn, who was the son of a marine biologist and Hubbs's friend, to accompany him on an aerial look at San Ignacio Lagoon. Some of the footage from that flight was used in the movie short, *Cruise of the Zaca*, (Warner Brothers, 1952).

The Hubbses began aerial surveys of Baja calving lagoons in 1952 with help from Gifford C. Ewing, Ph.D., an excellent pilot and a Scripps Institution physical oceanographer. On future trips Hubbs enlisted the help of Raymond M. Gilmore of the U.S. Fish & Wildlife Service, and later a research associate at the San Diego Natural History Museum. Hubbs and

Gilmore continued these aerial accounts through 1964. Not since the 1874 account by whaler Charles Melville Scammon in his book, *The Marine Mammals of the North-western Coast of North America*, had there been such substantial observations of the Gray Whales in the Baja lagoons.

Carl Hubbs's studies and research helped spark growing international efforts to save Gray Whales as well as other endangered marine mammals. Hubbs has been described as an "optimistic and diplomatic conservationist" who had great success in working with the Mexican government to establish a sanctuary for gray whales in the Baja lagoons. As early as 1956 Hubbs and Ewing began urging the Mexican government to establish the lagoons of Baja as sanctuaries for the Gray Whales.

In December 1971 Mexican President Luis Echeverria signed legislation that established the world's first whale reserve at *Ojo de Liebre*, a Gray Whale birthing lagoon north of *Laguna San Ignacio*. Less than a year later Echeverria declared both *Laguna San Ignacio* and *Ojo de Liebre* as Migratory Bird and Wildlife Refuges. Around the same time Raymond Gilmore made the bold suggestion that Mexico could make more money with whale watching rather than whale hunting. In those days the idea of whale watching as a successful business venture was in its infancy. These visionaries realized the whales were far more valuable alive, providing cultural and aesthetic enrichment as well as a strong source of revenue in an economically poor and isolated area of Baja. Gilmore once predicted, "The forces of conservation will meet the forces of exploitation head on. Let us hope that understanding prevails."

Creating El Vizcaíno Biosphere Reserve

In the 1970s and 1980s the Mexican Congress enacted many laws to increase protection of the Gray Whale. In 1977 Mexico sponsored the First International Symposium on the Gray Whale in *Guerrero Negro*.

At that meeting both researchers and policy makers from Mexico and the United States discussed the most effective ways to protect the Gray Whales in their continued population recovery. The symposium also addressed the conservation of the lagoon complex within the Vizcaíno Desert. In 1979 President José Lopez Portillo declared *Laguna San Ignacio* a Whale Refuge and Maritime Tourist Attraction Zone. During this time period the United States began passing legislation to protect marine life, including the Gray Whales. The Marine Mammal Act of 1972 and the Endangered Species Act of 1973 were significant actions taken by the United States to protect endangered species near extinction.

The first systematic study of Gray Whales in San Ignacio Lagoon began in 1984, led by U.S. researchers Mary Lou Jones and Steven Swartz. They wanted to provide baseline information on the breeding whales in San Ignacio Lagoon, and to evaluate the effects of whale watching activities within the lagoon. This field research took place over a five-year period, and generated important information on numbers and distribution of whales, specific location of the nursery areas, seasonal births, mortality rates, and the number of whale watching vessels and tourists at the lagoon with the whales. The result of their research along with contributions from other researchers was a six-hundred-page book, *The Gray Whale: Eschrichtius robustus* (Academic Press, 1984), edited by Jones and Swartz.

Ongoing efforts by Mexican biologists, naturalists, and environmentalists, supported by individuals and environmental groups outside of Mexico, culminated with President Miguel de la Madrid signing a decree for the establishment of El Vizcaíno Biosphere Reserve in November 1988. The reserve was named after Sebastian Vizcaíno, a Spanish Viceroy in Mexico City who was best known for the accuracy of his hand-drawn marine charts. In 1602 Vizcaíno led a treacherous expedition along the Pacific Coast that began in Acapulco and ended in Monterey Bay, which he charted and named. His maps were used for nearly two hundred years.

The establishment of this biosphere reserve was part of Mexico's vision to protect the whales as well as the Baja landscape. As of 2005 El Vizcaíno Biosphere Reserve encompasses 6,293,255 acres and includes *Ojo de Liebre*, *Guerrero Negro* and *Laguna Manuela* to the north, and *Laguna San Ignacio* to the south, then stretches from the Pacific side of the Baja Peninsula to the Sea of Cortez in the Gulf of California on the east side of Baja. The reserve also includes a strip of ocean along both coasts extending a little more than three miles (five kilometers) out from the coastlines.

El Vizcaíno Biosphere Reserve was created within the framework of Mexico's National System of Protected Areas. Most of these designated areas, including biosphere reserves, are managed by the *Comision Nacional de Areas Naturales Protegidas* (CONANP), Mexico's national park service. These reserves allow residents to continue to live in and use the natural resources in a protected natural area after its designation as a reserve. In addition to conducting biological surveys and ecological studies, CONANP encourages

Desert landscape surrounds the lagoon.

ROBIN KOBALY

research on sustainable resources for the local community to use as well as help them participate in wildlife protection. Mexico hopes the residents within these biosphere reserves will benefit from sustainable development, including ecotourism. However, designation of an area as a biosphere does not necessarily protect it from some types of development, such as homes

El Vizcaíno Biosphere Reserve on the Baja California Peninsula.

and businesses for the local residents. The development projects must be sustainable ones that are compatible with the objectives of the biosphere reserve.

Mexico then requested that portions of El Vizcaíno Biosphere Reserve, specifically *Laguna San Ignacio* and *Ojo de Liebre* be added to the World Heritage Site list of the United Nations Educational,

Scientific, and Cultural Organization (UNESCO). Mexico justified its request for adding the whale sanctuary to the World Heritage list because: "It is an outstanding example representing significant ongoing biological evolution . . . It contains unique and superlative natural features of exceptional beauty . . .[and] It contains the most important and significant habitats where threatened species of plants and animals still survive."

In 1993 UNESCO added the lagoons to its World Heritage Site list, noting: "What makes the concept of World Heritage exceptional is its universal application. World Heritage sites belong to all the peoples of the world, irrespective of the territory on which they are located." In that same year, the rock paintings of the *Sierra de San Francisco,* about sixty miles from San Ignacio Lagoon, were also noted as a World Heritage site.

Managed Whale Watching

Once the Mexican government established the Biosphere Reserve in 1988, Mexican naturalists and marine biologists carefully studied and planned for the best way to allow whale watching boats in the birthing lagoons. They were concerned that whale watching did not disturb mating and calving whales. Marine biologist José Ángel Sánchez Pacheco led this effort. He had also worked on establishing El Vizcaíno Biosphere Reserve.

In 1984 José was working for Mexico's environmental agency when he began his research to establish recommendations and guidelines for whale watching in the lagoons. The goal was to minimize impact on the whales and their habitat. "I tried to find answers to the everyday questions about the whales that I couldn't find in the literature," explains José about those early years. "With limited equipment and lots of time I began my research. First I studied the abundance of whales in the lagoons and their distribution. Then I studied the birth rate of calves in the lagoons, and the mortality rates." José then observed the impact of boats and whale watching itself on the whales. His field research took about ten years before he made his recommendations to the environmental agency. José determined how many boats could be on the lagoon at a given time, the whale watching boundaries, and guidelines for boaters when they were in the vicinity of whales. Based on José's recommendations, the El Vizcaíno Biosphere administration established the first guidelines for whale watching in *Laguna San Ignacio, Ojo de Liebre*, and *Bahia Magdelena.*

At the same time José was observing the whales, his colleague and friend, Ingeniero Alfredo Bermudez Almada, was working closely with the local fishing communities to give them information about the benefits of ecotourism and the potential economic gains from whale watching. At that time the local fishers were desperate to diversify their economic activity. José recalls, "It was difficult to convince some of the fishermen that whale watching was profitable in the short run, and in the long run. We also had to spend time reassuring some of the locals that the whales were not a problem, but an opportunity." Some of the locals did not like the idea of having fishing restrictions in the lagoon during whale watching season and they doubted the benefits of ecotourism. "Alfredo deserves a lot of the credit for the benefits the locals enjoy today from whale watching," notes José. "It took several meetings with fishermen, politicians, government officials, and the general public to provide them with lots of information on the benefits of whale watching. We also had to show them that in the end the regulations in the birthing lagoons would benefit the locals who could join the foreigners already making money on whale watching." Alfredo suffered a heart attack during one of the intense meetings at *Bahia Magdelena*, but he did recover to witness the results of his hard work—a successful ecotourism business for the locals in Baja's whale birthing lagoons.

More than two decades later José continues to visit *Laguna San Ignacio*, regularly, to monitor the continued workability of the regulations he established for successful whale watching. José knows the local fishermen and their families, and has a great respect for how well they manage their ecotourism businesses. One day while out on the lagoon, observing the whales and boats, he noted, "I helped determine the first regulations, but it doesn't mean that they should be set 'in stone.' The more we learn about the whales and the ongoing impact of our different activities, the more fine-tuning can be made. In the process it is important to take into account the socioeconomic needs of the locals." Overall he is pleased to see the whale watching plan work so well to the benefit of the whales and the local residents.

José also stays in contact with the Biosphere Reserve researchers and authorities to make sure they know that the decisions made in the past for establishing the current regulations were established for good reasons and a lot of work stands behind those decisions. José keeps up on the latest scientific information on Gray Whales, and he contributes to the growing bank of information with his own observations and writings.

José Ángel Sánchez Pacheco, Gray Whale researcher and naturalist, prepares to release a green sea turtle in the lagoon.

As of 2005 the current director of *El Vizcaíno Biosphere Reserve* is Benito Bermudez Almada, the younger brother of Ingenerio Alfredo Bermudez Almada. His job includes overseeing San Ignacio Lagoon activities throughout the year. There is also an official federal enforcement ranger from *Procuraduria Federal de Protecion Al Ambiente* (PROFEPA), which is the Federal Environmental Protection Agency. PROFEPA is the enforcement arm of the Ministry for the Environment, Natural Resources, and Fisheries (SEMARNAP). The casual visitor to San Ignacio Lagoon has no idea of the tremendous research and organization that went into establishing the whale watching system, perhaps because it works so smoothly.

The Ejidos *and the Land Owners*

The million acres of land that surround San Ignacio Lagoon are divided into six *ejidos*, which are communal landholding groups. Much of Mexico's territory is divided into *ejidos*, the result of the Mexican government's decision in 1917 to form communal landholdings. Mexico's Constitution provided for the government to divide and distribute land to peasant collectives while retaining ownership of the land and preventing its sale. When the *ejidos* were first established, they provided land for a community of farmers, ranchers, and fishers to produce food by using funds provided by the Mexican government. In turn, the government would then buy the products to supply urban areas with food and to export to other countries.

Part of the plan to create *ejidos* was to break up huge land grants inherited by descendants of the Spanish conquerors when Mexico was a Spanish colony. Owners of these expansive land holdings usually had hundreds of *campesinos* (peasants) under their rule, working the land like indentured servants, entrenched in poverty with no hope of improving their lives. In those days, Baja must have seemed a far-off, desolate place, but with the promise of owning land, some people migrated to Baja to form an *ejido*.

From 1934 to 1940 under the presidency of Lázaro Cárdenas, the *ejidos* became more established throughout Baja. At that time people involved with the *ejidos* were not allowed to sell their land, but they could work it to make a living. Some were fortunate with the location of their property within an *ejido* and they could make a living by farming or fishing. But for others the Baja landscape was too harsh and after living in poverty for generations, they went to mainland Mexico, leaving their co-op share of the *ejido* behind.

Over time some of the *ejidos* became uninhabited and eventually new-comers arrived to claim some of those vacant *ejidos*, seeing the potential for opportunities. The new residents would officially claim ownership in an *ejido* by filling out the required paperwork and submitting their applications to the Mexican government. This is where land ownership becomes vague in Baja. It was confusing for many longtime residents on rural *ejidos* because they did not understand the importance of registering required government

Local fisherman tends the air supply line for the diver below gathering scallops with hookah gear in the shallows of the lagoon.

ROBIN KOBALY

paperwork to establish their ownership in an *ejido*. They had always lived on the land, sometimes for many generations, and the laws of the federal government were not part of their rural life. These people lived by the tides, the wind, and weather, and focused on caring for their families—not the laws established by a government in distant Mexico City. In addition, until recent years, the telegraph was the only major way to communicate. Even today, most rural areas do not have phones or mail service.

For many decades, *ejido* land could not be sold or purchased. However, amendments to the Mexican constitution in 1992 allowed tenants of *ejidos* to parcelize the community property and sell the land on which they resided if they decided or if the community ruling the *ejido* approved of the sale. Now, *ejidal* lands are categorized as private parcels and common use lands. This is now happening throughout the Baja California peninsula. The change in the law has opened the doors to potential developers who entice owners of *ejiditos* (small parcels of land) located within an *ejido* with offers to buy their land, allowing private development. However, the new law also gives *ejidos* the power to sell conservation easements with the goal of restricting development.

San Ignacio Lagoon's Ejidos

At San Ignacio Lagoon the *ejidos* surrounding the lagoon have not been subdivided into individual parcels, although that threat presently exists. There is an organized effort to conserve the San Ignacio Wetlands Complex, which is mostly owned by *ejidos*. Many local *ejido* leaders are working with several conservation groups in Mexico and the United States to find ways to restrict development on their communally owned land while at the same time establishing areas for economic uses that are low impact. The key organizations involved in this complex and international effort include Pronatura, Mexico's prominent environmental group; WILDCOAST, an international conservation team focused on protecting coastal communities; the International Community Foundation (ICF), a public charity focused on benefiting under-served communities; the Natural Resources Defense Council (NRDC), a U.S.-based nonprofit dedicated to protecting public health and the environment; *Laguna Baja Asociación Rural de Interés Colectivo* (ARIC), a coalition of nine, small-scale ecotourism enterprises operating in *Laguna San Ignacio;* and the *Ejido Luis Echeverría*, the leading *ejido* in San Ignacio Lagoon that has been instrumental in defending *Laguna San Ignacio* from large-scale development threats. All of these groups have joined together to form the *Laguna San Ignacio* Conservation Alliance (LSIC).

The LSIC mission is to work with community-based organizations and private landowners within the *Laguna San Ignacio* Wetland Complex to protect one-million acres of pristine coastal eco-systems. The LSIC is establishing the first legal conservation agreements in Mexico with integrated legal defense fund accounts. The ongoing efforts for conservation of the *Laguna San Ignacio* Wetland Complex involves players at the community, local, regional, national, and international levels. This is not an easy goal to accomplish but definitely one well worth the efforts.

Some of the *ejidos* have received outside offers from developers to buy parcels of land. The ARIC, mostly comprised of local fisherman at San Ignacio Lagoon, have met with *ejido* members from the *Ejido San Ignacio* and the *Ejido Emiliano Zapata* to discuss conservation and alternatives to development interests knocking on their door.

An Ejido *Votes for Conservation*

A major step toward protecting San Ignacio Lagoon took place in October 2005. Members of the *Ejido Luis Echeverría* unanimously agreed to limit development on their property in exchange for an annual payment of $25,000 in perpetuity to be used as seed money for low-impact development projects. There is a separate agreement where members will split a one-time payment of $545,000 to preserve the other 20,000 acres they hold as individuals. This decision by *Ejido Luis Echeverría* has made it a conservation leader in Baja California.

Upon signing the agreement, Raúl López Góngora, president of the *ejido,* stated that this agreement is historic because it shows the efforts "to see conservation as an opportunity for development." Though conservation easements, or private land trusts, have been negotiated with other *ejidos*, this agreement is the first time that an *ejido's* entire territory has come under private protection.

Pronatura will monitor the agreement, and the ICF based in San Diego will maintain the trust fund. The LSICA hopes to eventually negotiate with the five other *ejidos* to protect all of the land surrounding the lagoon. The goal is to set a prec-edent for conservation of this region through low-impact ecotourism with whale watching being the

Raúl López Góngora, president of Ejido Luis Echeverría

cornerstone. Making a living on the sparse Baja landscape is tough and money is scarce for most of the residents. For the *ejidos* to have a say in their futures is beneficial, particularly if they can improve their lives and protect their environment.

The ongoing threat is the potential for many locals to sell their parcels (*ejiditos*) for small amounts of money, not realizing the value of what they have. However, with good guidance this can be avoided and the future of *ejido* members protected. The recent agreement reached by members of the *Ejido Luis Echeverría* and conservation groups is hope-ful. There are about five hundred people living in *Ejido Luis Echeverría* and about forty-three are voting members. These *ejido* members under-stand how important it is for the local community to thrive while at the same time being attentive to conservation. It took more than ten years for this *ejido* to organize and build consensus to work as a community.

Raúl was a young college graduate with expertise as a fisheries engineer when the Mexican government sent him to Baja in 1983 to help organize fishing cooperatives. "I am part of a generation that is really concerned about social problems," explained Raúl, 44, in a 2006 interview. "We care about conservation." He noted their efforts toward this goal greatly improved with establishment of the Biosphere Reserve. "This changed things and kept the lagoon from becoming a disaster."

Today *Ejido Luis Echeverría* focuses on many aspects of the community in addition to conservation efforts. The community offers high school scholarships with its program, *Patronato del Estudiante Lagunero*, understanding the importance of educating future leaders. A community art group was started by Teresa de Varela who is an artist, teacher, and member of the music group, Gitanos. Teresa began organizing the local art cooperative, *Mar Azul*, in 2002. Her vision is to help community members develop art skills and find ways to use available materials to create art for tourists visiting the lagoon as well as for regional markets. With the help of a grant, members of the art co-operative are building a community art studio for locals to work and display their art for sale. As of 2006 about fifteen locals are working with the art co-op, including a couple of former fishermen. Deborah Maciel Dominguez, one of the first to join the art coop and president of the organization, now has her husband, Luis Romero Marron, working with the group. Together they make more money creating art than from fishing. "Fishing is difficult for these people," Teresa explained, understanding the importance of diversifying economic opportunities in the area. "Fishing is getting harder every year. If the people don't stay here, the government isn't going to protect the lagoon. The people that grew up here and live here and love this community—they are the ones who are going to protect this area."

Members of *Ejido Luis Echeverría* are also looking for ways to help local ranchers who want to maintain their cultural connection to the

Visitors kayak in the mangroves along the southern shore of San Ignacio Lagoon.

ROBIN KOBALY

ROBIN KOBALY

Local school at El Centro *in* Ejido Luis Echeverría

land. It is difficult for ranchers to prosper in a desert environment and still be attentive to conservation since food for cattle is always a challenge. Recently, the *ejido* began building community green houses that will produce up to ten tons of food a month to feed cows and goats. "One of the successes of the *ejido* is that our minds are changing," Raúl proudly explained. "We are now looking for ways to make our efforts environmentally friendly." They also want to plan and develop enough tourist activity to ensure that ecotourism continues to be a viable livelihood at the lagoon. "We believe we have to control the development of the area," he added, noting the *ejido's* recent decision for conservation. "That's how the *ejido* can guarantee the visitors to the lagoon that they will have the same opportunity for a nice time."

The question remains how the residents of San Ignacio Lagoon can continue to make money, improve their lives, and create security for their families while at the same time protecting this unique environment surrounding the last pristine birthing lagoon for Gray Whales.

Threats to the Lagoon

In recent times one of the biggest environmental threats to the lagoon took place in the 1990s. Mitsubishi Corporation proposed to build a large industrial salt evaporation facility adjacent to San

Ignacio Lagoon, which would have adversely affected this last pristine calving lagoon. Mitsubishi already owns a salt mining facility at *Laguna Guerrero Negro* and wanted to expand. In 1994 the Mexican Ministry of Trade and Mitsubishi began negotiations for a joint venture without making their plans known to the public. The Mexican environmental organization, *Grupo de los Cien* (Group of 100), alerted the international community to the threat. It became a rallying point for environmental groups and concerned individuals worldwide, in particular the Natural Resources Defense Council (NRDC).

The main reason Mitsubishi had a chance for succeeding with this proposal was because of new laws that allowed *ejidos* to sell their land. Mitsubishi had promised many things that would make the locals' lives easier, but in reality critics believed these were empty promises. Diligent work by individuals and environmental groups helped stop this potential ecological disaster and alert local residents to be wary. After years of outcry from the international environmental community as well as thousands of individuals, the Mitsubishi project was stopped. However, this does not preclude another attempt in the future. As author and environmental journalist, Dick Russell, astutely wrote in a magazine article, "A spirited campaign by Mexican and American environmental groups ultimately scuttled the project, but recent talk of its revival brings realization that vigilance—not victory—is all that can ever really be declared."

Now, the greatest threat looming over San Ignacio Lagoon, and the entire Baja Peninsula is a tourism project in the makings since the 1970s. Mexico's tourism promotion agency, the National Tourism Fund (FONATUR), has proposed a complex and multi-layered development plan along the Baja Peninsula called *La Escalera Nauticá* (Nautical Stairs) project. This plan came out of meetings by a panel of

ROBIN KOBALY

Cormorants perch in mangroves on the southern shore of San Ignacio Lagoon.

international investors who met to speculate on major development throughout the Baja California Peninsula.

If the project were to be completely developed this would include the creation of ten new ports; expansion of twelve existing ports and twenty existing airports or airfields; and development of a network of roads and highways throughout Baja. Basically, the project plans would develop a chain of twenty-four marinas to provide North American yachters a long journey filled with tourist attractions, golf courses, hotels, and real estate developments. FONATUR envisions this project attracting about 52,000 yachts and one million visitors annually throughout Baja; however, an independent international estimate concluded that FONATUR had overestimated the market by 600 percent.

In 2003 the environmental group, Pro Peninsula, published an extensive and startling report on this proposed development called "Sustainable Coastal Development: *La Escalera Náutica,* A Mega-tourism Project on the Baja California Peninsula." This report compiles information on this proposed development so individuals, organizations, and communities can be informed and get involved in promoting the best interests of Baja "in a sustainable manner."

One of the proposed marinas would be situated just north of San Ignacio Lagoon at *Punta Abreojos*, which is also within El Vizcaíno Biosphere Reserve. This is a small fishing village with less than one thousand residents and home to the *Abreojos* fishing co-operative. The co-op has been very successful with its fishing endeavors and in recent years has undertaken an environmentally sustainable aquaculture project focused on oyster production.

Future development is uncertain at *Punta Abreojos*, however, the local environmental organization, *Comité Abreojeño para la Defensa de los Recursos Naturales de Bahía Ballenas* (CADERNABB) is keeping a close watch on any proposed future development in *Punta Abreojos*. In addition, the LSICA is vigilantly watching this project and attempts by the Mexican government and international big business to steamroll over the Baja Peninsula with *Escalera Nauticá*. For example, a coalition of environmental groups eventually reached an agreement with FONATUR officials who agreed to scale back the project and only promote existing marina upgrades under the banner of *Programa Mar de Cortez*. FONATUR breached this agreement when it announced plans for new marinas in the Sea of Cortez and the Pacific Ocean, including the recent marina approval for *Punta Abreojos*. Interestingly, a report on the LSICA website states a number of FONATUR maps show the marina in the exact location that had been proposed for the Mitsubishi salt project's 1.2-mile pier.

On multiple levels the *Escalera Náutica Project* could adversely affect the entire Baja landscape as well as its communities and towns. As of 2006 no site specific Environmental Impact Assessments (EIAs) have been submitted. At this point the Mexican government has not involved the citizens of Baja in its project decision-making. This could be disastrous for Baja's people and culture. As the authors, Kama Dean and Chris Pesenti, state in their report, "Many are also concerned with the social impacts of the project. Some fear that the rural population will be turned into a labor force for tourists. Locals living in coastal areas on the peninsula exist as fishermen and ecotourism guides. Most have no desire to give up their traditional way of life to serve tourists."

There is also the fear that communities and fishermen will be displaced to make room for development, as was the case in Hualtuco (today a resort town in the southern state of Oaxaca). Many of the project plans for development released by FONATUR include development where homes and community buildings currently exist, pointing to the possibility of expropriation of lands. According to one author, "The project threatens to tear apart the social and cultural fabric of the region."

Vigilance

Vigilance will always be necessary for the protection of San Ignacio Lagoon and the whales. During the Mitsubishi salt plant battle environmental journalist Dick Russell wrote passionately about preserving San Ignacio Lagoon. What he wrote in the 1990s still holds true in this new century as another project threatens San Ignacio Lagoon and the greater Baja landscape.

> Which brings us, once more, to the gray whale, the whale that despite our history in seeking to destroy it, wants to live closest to us. If they are being forgiving toward us, the implications are enormous. This is surely, in part, why they touch us so deeply. Like gray whales in their lagoons, human beings too must seek solace, a centering focal point, a place to go that remains relatively untouched and pure. A place to remind ourselves of our basic nature, not surrounded by all we have built. So do we commune with the whales at San Ignacio.

PART TWO

The Whales

Gray Whales

ARTWORK BY J.D. MAYHEW

SIX

A Brief History
of Whale Hunting

*A*s a young college student I often was outraged at the foibles of humanity. A wise history professor at that time cautioned not to judge the past too harshly. When students voiced their youthful anger at sins of the past, he would calmly reply, "People made the best decisions they could with the information they had at the time."

Perhaps that was the most important lesson I learned in my history course. Even today, more than thirty years later I try to hold on to my professor's perspective, especially when considering the history of whaling and the massive commercial slaughter of whales and other marine mammals. Intense commercial whaling lasted for about five hundred years and left most whale populations decimated. Whaling was once considered an admirable livelihood providing an essential commodity—oil. Injuries and death were common among whalers but the commercial value of whale products kept hunters pursuing the largest living creatures until public outcry worldwide halted the near demise of whale populations.

Thanks to international efforts most whales are protected today, yet there is an ongoing struggle from some nations eager to return to whaling. And there are a few nations that continue to hunt whales, defying international agreements to ban whale hunting. The future of whales is fragile, dependent on human decisions and what world opinion regards as valuable.

The first whale hunters

Archaeological evidence indicates that as early as five thousand years ago, people from the extreme northern latitudes of what is now Alaska, Norway, and Canada may have used whales for food, and other necessities. They took advantage of any marine mammals stranded on their shores. Once humans discovered the value of whales their scavenging expanded to hunting by deliberately driving whales on shore, and then killing them.

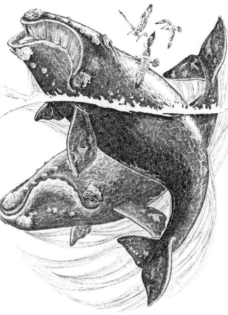

Right Whales
ARTWORK BY J.D. MAYHEW

It is impossible to give an exact date when humans first hunted whales. The Inuit lived in the most extreme northern latitude, and were among the first people to successfully hunt whales. They hunted Gray, Bowhead, and Right Whales, which were easier to hunt from canoes and dugouts than most whales because they traveled so slowly. The Inuit hunted whales for the meat and blubber, and used the huge whale bones to make sleds and structures for their skin-covered summer dwellings. The whale provided the Inuit with a rich resource for survival in a challenging Arctic habitat.

Archaeologists and historians attribute the first recorded whale hunts on the high seas to the Norse Vikings of Scandinavia around 800 A.D. Other peoples worldwide were hunting whales at this time, but these hunts were mostly small and close to home to provide what the tribe or band of people needed. Pacific Northwest Native Americans such as the Makah and Quileute, whose tribal lands are situated on what is now the northern shoreline of Washington state, claim a long history of whale hunting that dates back fifteen hundred years or more. The Japanese also claim a long tradition of whaling.

The first commercial whaling in Europe began during the ninth century. People of the Basque region from northern Spain and southern France learned the value of whale hunting from Norse whalers, who had traveled the North Atlantic in their pursuit of whales. The Basques hunted the Northern Right Whales, Bowhead Whales, and Gray Whales. In particular, the Basques hunted Right Whales, who got their name from whalers identifying them as the "right" whales because they were the easiest to hunt. In addition, Right Whales tended to float longer after killed, making it easier to strip the blubber and skin from the carcasses alongside the ship. This was called flensing the whale. Right Whales are more than fifty-feet long, and weigh more than forty tons, providing whalers with ample "product" in a highly profitable trade, primarily to France and Spain.

The Basques were the first to create a whaling industry and were whaling at the Newfoundland Banks by 1372, according to the National Maritime Museum. The Basques followed Right Whales into the Bay of Biscay off the northwest coast of France and the northern coast of Spain where the whales birthed their young. With this type of aggressive hunting, the Basques had hunted the Northern Right Whale to near depletion in this area by the fifteenth century. Whalers then extended their hunting to the north and used bigger merchant ships known as carracks, which were roughly sixty-five feet long and sat high in the water.

Historian Joe C. Flatman has studied Medieval maritime life by examining numerous manuscript illuminations and artistic renderings

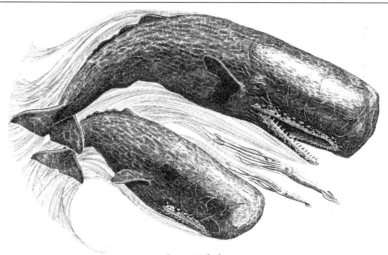

Sperm Whales
ARTWORK BY J.D. MAYHEW

in British and French libraries. By studying these renderings, Flatman has gathered additional, unknown historic information about Medieval life. He found iconographic evidence in artists' maritime renderings that suggest whales and dolphins were thought to be lured to ships by whalers playing music, specifically from a hurdy-gurdy. In his writings Flatman notes, "This practice was thought to have been inspired by the classical Greek notion that dolphins are susceptible to music."

By the end of the sixteenth century English merchant ships sailed to the Arctic region hunting whales. The British colonies in North America, later to become the United States, established their first whaling port in 1650 in Nantucket, Massachusetts. Within twenty years Yankee whalers flourished as the demand for precious whale oil and whale products exploded. They began to hunt a previously feared whale, the Sperm Whale, which lived off the East Coast of the United States. Sperm Whales are sixty feet long, have teeth, can dive deep for long periods of time, and hunt for their food instead of grazing. When these mighty whales were plentiful they traveled in pods with hundreds of family members, living in deep waters usually seven or more miles off shore. Previously, when whalers sighted groups of Sperm Whales they would turn and run, the hunt too risky. But in the early 1700s Yankee whalers began hunting Sperm Whales for their plentiful and superior oil. One Sperm Whale could provide up to 50 barrels, or 2,000 gallons of oil.

There were many uses for the parts of a whale, but the most important product was oil extracted from blubber. People used whale oil for lamps and candles as well as for soaps, margarine, cooking fats, crayons, paints, and glycerin. They rendered baleen for use in umbrellas, whips, crinolines, corset stays, and other items of clothing. Consumers wanted baleen or "whalebone" because boiled baleen was pliant and easy to shape. They would mold the baleen while it was wet and it would retain the bend or mold once dried.

Carvers used real whalebones to create decorative items, and leather workers used whale skin for bootlaces or leather-like items. Sperm Whale teeth became the palette for an American folk art, scrimshaw. Whalers often spent many idle hours at sea, so they began creating images in black ink or "lamp-black" on whales' teeth.

European and American whalers usually did not eat whale meat, but they did use it for fertilizer or animal food. It was not uncommon for these whalers to simply throw away whale meat. On whaling expeditions to the polar regions, hunters also hunted walrus, penguins, and polar bears.

When whalers sighted a whale, sailors quickly lowered boats into the water. Each boat carried a harpooner, who was in command, and six to seven men who rowed. When the boat was in a position to strike or what the whalers called "on fish," the harpooner would drive his harpoon into the back of the whale, just behind the blowhole. The harpoon was not intended to kill the whale, but to attach a rope to the whale's body. The wounded whale would then drag the boat until exhausted, which was a very dangerous time for the crew. Whale boats were frequently upset by whales thrashing about after they had been harpooned. If a whale "sounded," diving deep, then the harpooner would have to cut the line immediately or face disaster. If the whale continued to swim along the water's surface until exhausted, the whalers would move in for the kill.

Whalers then hauled the dead whale alongside their ship. The men would flense the whale by cutting long strips called "blanket pieces" from the carcass and haul them by block and tackle onto the deck. A blanket piece was then cut into small blocks and melted in heated iron pots known as "try-works." Heating produced whale oil, later stored in casks in the hull of the ship.

By the seventeenth century, Britain, Holland, Germany, and France had embarked on their own whaling industries, sailing to new areas of the world. Not surprisingly, by the eighteenth century along the coasts of Spain, Portugal, and France, the whales had been hunted so extensively only small numbers remained. But England bore the greatest responsibility for the demise of great whale populations in northern waters during this time. In only a few decades the British Empire's rise in power and its superior ships allowed English whalers to take everything in their path. Whalers had to move their hunting range to new areas in the open seas still teaming with new populations of Bowheads, Humpbacks, and Right Whales.

In the New World, Yankee whalers were busy. Shore-hugging whales such as Gray Whales were always the first to be hunted down. Gray Whales once roamed the Atlantic Ocean as well as the Pacific, but by 1750 colonial records indicate that the Atlantic Gray Whale had been annihilated off the East coast of the United States. Gray Whales also had disappeared from European waters. The Atlantic Gray became the first whale population to be hunted to extinction.

Bowhead Whales, with smaller Beluga Whales
ARTWORK BY J.D. MAYHEW

By the nineteenth century American whalers led the slaughter worldwide. By 1830 seventy-two whaling ships sailed from Nantucket each year, returning with more than thirty thousand barrels of whale oil for international export. This translated into millions of dollars of profits, primarily for the owners of the whaling ships.

In the following ten years, the growth of the American whaling industry outgrew Nantucket, and New Bedford became the supreme whaling port. From 1843 on, the United States was unrivaled in the whaling industry worldwide. During this time there were 882 whaling ships around the world and 652 were from America. Before long this over-hunting of whales would take a grisly toll.

The Advent of Modern Whaling

Whales might have survived the incredible onslaught of commercial whaling if two innovations of the second half of the nineteenth century had not changed the plight of the whale forever. In 1868 the Norwegian whaler, Svend Foyn, developed the explosive grenade harpoon and the cannon for firing it. Foyn built his whaling invention on the earlier experiments of the American whaler Tomas Welcome Roys. This new invention allowed whalers to fire the harpoon from a large gun mounted on the bow of the main vessel. It could travel more than one hundred fifty feet with fairly good accuracy and it exploded on impact. A star-shaped barb opened and broke a vial of sulphuric acid that caused a powder chamber to catch fire. This new approach made it much harder for a whale to escape, and the number of whales slaughtered each year rapidly increased.

During this same time period the whalers' sailing ships were being replaced by the newly designed and much faster steam-driven vessels. These faster ships could travel further and fire exploding harpoons from greater distances, reducing the danger to whalers while killing more whales. After that, the whales never had a chance.

These advances in modern whaling led to factory ships equipped with ramps or slipways for hauling the whales onboard after one or two exploding harpoons hit the mark. Powerful winches hauled the dead whale up the slipway onto the ship's deck for flensing. Now ships could

Blue Whales
ARTWORK BY J.D. MAYHEW

handle functions at sea that whalers traditionally executed at shore-based stations. The grisly, bloody process of butchering thousands of whales became something few people witnessed.

Within a matter of years these inventions made it possible to find and hunt quicker-moving whales in places previously too remote for whaling. The new whaling technology could now exploit the species-rich Antarctic Ocean, the richest area left on earth for the great whales who remained. Antarctica provided vast feeding areas for the endangered Blue, Fin, and Sei Whales, as well as for other species who still flourished.

Scammon and the Slaughter of Gray Whales

A well-known Yankee whaling captain, Charles Melville Scammon, found the birthing lagoons of Baja, Mexico with the help of reports from Baja locals who talked about lagoons packed with whales. In December 1857 a lookout on Scammon's whaling ship, *Boston,* sighted whale spouts that looked as if they were coming from sand dunes along the Baja coastline. When Scammon first approached the lagoon, *Ojo de Liebre,* he did not try to navigate his way in, but sent for a shallow-draft schooner, a smaller whaleboat. Within the lagoon he found thousands of Gray Whales, primarily mothers and their babies. With this, the violent slaughter in the Baja whale nurseries began, led by Scammon, and quickly followed by other Yankee whalers. He did not visit all of the Baja lagoons, but was given credit for discovering them. *Ojo de Liebre* was later referred to as "Scammon's Lagoon"—a rather unfitting tribute to the man who brought such killing and destruction to a once peaceful area.

Whalers systematically reduced the Gray Whale population every year. They could easily predict the Gray Whales' migration patterns because the Grays swam near the coast and returned every year to

Fin Whales
ARTWORK BY J.D. MAYHEW

specific areas to mate and birth. This migratory pattern made it possible for whalers to invade the Gray Whales' birthing lagoons along Baja, or patiently wait just outside of the lagoons where they could easily hunt thousands of whales.

After he stopped whaling, Scammon wrote about his eight years as a whaler, describing his accounts of those whaling days and his observations of the whales he hunted. He wrote short articles about his adventures and they were published in the *Overland Monthly*, a well-respected magazine in San Francisco. Scammon also wrote a book, *Marine Mammals of the Northeastern Coast of North America*, published in 1874. It sold poorly, however, he was a keen observer of nature and history, and his writings and artwork represented the best knowledge of whales for almost fifty years.

In his book Scammon describes the hunt in unemotional terms, yet reading his passages reveals some of the haunting tragedies of whaling. Perhaps one of the most difficult to reconcile is his description of baby whales he calls "cubs" after the slaughter of their mothers. Scammon wrote:

> It is true that instances have occurred where two, three or more cubs have been seen with one California Gray Whale; but this has only happened in the lagoons where there had been great slaughter among the cows, leaving their young ones motherless, so that these straggle about sometimes following other whales, sometime clustering by themselves a half-dozen together....When the mother was taken to the ship to be cut in, the young one followed and remained for about two weeks; but whether it lived to come to maturity is a matter of conjecture.

Once whalers had killed the mother whales, the baby whales would circle the ship for days looking for their mothers. Eventually the orphaned calves died of starvation. Scammon was mistaken when he suggested mother whales might also care for orphaned calves. A mother whale cannot nurse more than one baby at a time. This haunting scenario was played out countless times in a whaling season as whalers indiscriminately killed whales, including nursing mothers. At the time Scammon wrote about his whaling accounts, this same sad story was being played out thousands of times worldwide, as it had over the past nine hundred years of whaling. Sadly, this scenario continues in areas of the world where modern whalers still kill whales with nursing young, or pregnant whales. A Japanese government report revealed that in its 2006 whale hunt in the Antarctic, 70 percent of the whales hunted were pregnant: of 391 Minke Whales hunted, 294 were pregnant. Japanese whalers also hunted ten Fin Whales—listed as an endangered species—two of which were pregnant.

In his book Scammon also described the devastation left in the wake of intense whaling. He wrote about the large bays and lagoons where the Gray Whales congregated as "already nearly deserted" by the time he had stopped whaling. And as if acknowledging the irreparable damage from the whalers' indiscriminate slaughter of the Gray Whale, Scammon predicted in his book: "...and ere long it may be questioned whether this mammal will not be numbered among the extinct species of the Pacific."

After years of slaughtering whales in the Baja lagoons, whalers eventually stopped because the whales had been hunted so extensively it was no longer profitable to travel such a long distance in pursuit. There may have been more than twenty thousand California Gray Whales during the early 1850s, but within twenty years probably less than two thousand remained.

The International Whaling Commission

The rise of modern commercial whaling was short lived. There simply were not enough whales to support it. Factory ships were introduced to whaling in the 1920s and this allowed whalers to kill and process much greater numbers of whales. From the Artic to the Antarctic, whalers hunted males and females, juveniles and adults, using faster ships, newer weapons, and the latest technology. SONAR or SOund NAvigation and Ranging was first used during World War I to detect submarines. By the 1920s, Japan had adapted this technology for tracking the whale's direction and the distance from their boats.

By 1931 whale killing peaked with estimates between 44,000 and 55,000 whales slaughtered. In that year alone whalers massacred more than thirty thousand Blue Whales, the largest creature with perhaps the largest brain ever known to have lived on earth. International concern grew over hunting whales into extinction. Outcry from citizens worldwide continued to mount, as people began to realize that it was not long before several species of whales would be extinct, including the Pacific Gray Whales.

In response the League of Nations, the forerunner of the United Nations, formally recognized the worldwide threat to whales. In 1931 member nations drew up the the first international effort to protect whales, the Convention for the Regulation of Whaling. This first attempt did not hold much influence and at best, offered only partial protection, yet it was significant because the international community formally recognized the imminent threat to whales. One of the main goals of this international effort was to protect the most endangered species of the time—Pacific Gray Whales, Bowhead Whales, and Right Whales. In 1937 these three whales were the first to be listed for protection under the International Agreement for the Regulation of Whaling by the League of Nations.

World War II broke out in 1939 in Europe, and after the bombing of Pearl Harbor on December 7, 1941, the United States was fully engaged in the war, fighting both Germany and Japan. While humans fought the deadliest and largest continuous global war in human history, most of the whales of the world got a reprieve as humans focused their ships and guns on each other.

In 1946, one year after the end of World War II, whaling resumed. That same year a full International Convention for the Regulation of Whaling was ratified by more than sixty countries and the first ever International Whaling Commission (IWC) met. The IWC was not a conservation group as much as it was a group of whaling nations and whalers wanting to make sure they could continue hunting whales in some kind of orderly fashion and maintain their whaling industry. Most whaling nations recognized that in a few years there would no longer be whales to hunt if they all continued their indiscriminate hunting, going after the last remaining pockets of whales.

In the 1950s a small group of individuals organized the first whale watching boat tours off the Southern California coast. The idea of watching whales instead of hunting them would become a popular

Humpback Whales and Dolphins
ARTWORK BY J.D. MAYHEW

tourist activity that would take off in the 1970s and greatly influence future treatment of the remaining whales.

Just as whale watching in the United States began to flourish, U.S. whaling was coming to an end. In 1971 U.S. whalers killed their last whale, a Sperm Whale swimming just beyond the Golden Gate Bridge. They hauled the whale to the Del Monte Whaling rendering plant at Point Richmond in San Francisco Bay, ending a devastating chapter in U.S. whaling. By this time, the United States hunted whales primarily for use in dog food. That same year the U.S. federal government passed the Marine Mammal Protection Act of 1972, which protected whales, dolphins, seals, and all other marine mammals.

For more than thirty years the IWC had wrangled with ways to protect the remaining whales while at the same time sanctioning whaling. The IWC called these plans "Management Schemes," but they were flawed and mostly ineffective. But as the IWC became more influential in the conservation of whales, more of the open seas became off limits. An ongoing worldwide outcry against the slaughter of whales led to the IWC deciding to enforce a five-year whaling ban beginning in 1986.

The catch limits for all commercial whaling were set to zero, and the ban prohibited for-profit killing of ten whale species. They included Blue, Bowhead, Fin, Gray, Humpback, Minke, Pygmy Right, Sei, Right, and Sperm Whales.

Modern Whale Hunters

Unfortunately, the IWC left huge loopholes in this ban, in particular the provision that allows a country to conduct "scientific research" by killing a "limited" number of whales a year. Despite this ban, Norway and Japan continued whaling under the IWC provision for "scientific whaling." The Japanese hunted almost two thousand Minke Whales in 1987, according to Japan's government reports. Every year since the 1986 ban on whale hunting Japan has hunted Minke Whales. In 1994 Norway defied the ban and openly returned to commercial whaling, which it was allowed to do because it filed an official objection when the moratorium was first put in place. Norway continues to hunt Minke Whales in the North Atlantic Ocean for commercial purposes. In 2004 the World Wildlife Fund (WWF), a nonprofit organization dedicated to protecting wildlife, announced that well over 25,000 whales had been killed by Japan and Norway since 1986. This estimate does not include nursing calves who died after their mothers were slaughtered.

Japan in particular has taken advantage of the scientific loophole to continue its whaling practices. Japan and more recently, Iceland, claim they are killing whales for scientific purposes in order to study "stomach contents," "feeding habits," or "the impact of whales on the ocean ecosystem." These countries assert that studying what whales eat will help prove the unsubstantiated theory that these animals are consuming the world's fish stocks. Environmental organizations opposed to Japan's continued whaling decry this loophole of scientific research as irrelevant and useless, and nothing more than a thin disguise for commercial whaling.

In 2005 Japan made about $26.5 million by selling approximately 4.16 million pounds of whale meat to its restaurants and grocery stores—meat from whales killed for scientific research. That year Japan sent a fleet of fast, modern whaling ships to the oceans of Antarctica to hunt 850 Minke whales, considered "near threatened" by the World Conservation Union, and ten Fin Whales, the second largest of all whales, and an endangered species.

Environmental groups and IWC members opposed to Japan's pursuit of reinstating whale hunting question the reasons behind Japan's heavily subsidized whaling industry and its tactics of paying millions of dollars to other IWC member countries to vote for resumption of whale hunting. In recent years Japan has vociferously defended its right to hunt whales, claiming whale meat is an integral part of its culture. *Los Angeles Times* staff writers attending the 2006 IWC meeting in St. Kitts in the Eastern Caribbean reported that despite Japan's efforts to reintroduce whale meat into the Japanese diet, most consumers were not interested. "The whale meat diet is becoming more and more obsolete in Japan," said Junko Sakuma, an anti-whaling activist and author of a report that used statistics from Japan's fisheries agency to show unsold whale meat is piling up in industrial freezers.

Another important concern about the resumption of whale hunting is the question posed by health researchers who are advising against the consumption of whale meat because of the high level of toxins. Dr. Roger Payne at the Whale Conservation Institute, who has been studying and documenting whales since the 1970s, reports that chemicals have made their way up the food chain and into whales. "Unfortunately," said Dr. Payne, "the chemical revolution of the last century has produced synthetic contaminants not found in nature, to use in a range of pesticides, fertilizers, and other products. These substances wash from the land into the sea. Endocrine disrupting compounds are highly toxic, chemically stable, and long lived. They are also usually far more soluble in fats than water."

In May 2003 Norwegian scientists dealt a blow to the whale hunting industry when they advised pregnant women and nursing mothers to not eat whale meat because of the high levels of toxic mercury. Whales are susceptible to a build-up of toxins like mercury and PCBs because they live long lives and the poisons get lodged in their flesh and fat. Health warnings describe whale meat and blubber as a toxic mix that consumers need to be warned about. There is particular concern when the Japanese government encourages the use of whale meat for school children's lunches.

An Uncertain Future

The IWC's moratorium on whaling initiated in 1986 continues to be enforced based on a yearly vote by IWC members, which averages about sixty-six nations. In 2006 the majority of IWC members once again voted for the moratorium, however, Japan had one small victory. By one vote Japan got the IWC to pass "The St. Kitts Declaration," which calls on the IWC to return to its 1946 beginnings and concentrate solely on issues related to the regulation of commercial whaling. In 2007, Japan plans to add Humpback Whales, known for their complex and beautiful singing, to its list of whales to hunt.

In recent years the IWC turned its attention to the popular and expanding whale watching industry worldwide. IWC members first noticed the whale watching business in 1983 and a year later established a Whale Watching Working Group to discuss the benign use of whales and smaller cetaceans. The IWC is a body of nations fueled by the idea of making money on whales, and the fact that the members are taking steps to consider whale watching rather than whale hunting offers a glimmer of hope. However, after the 2006 meeting, whale conservationists and environmentalists see Japan's success with "The St. Kitts Declaration" as a wake-up call. Only by the slimmest of margins does the international community agree to stop hunting whales.

While the IWC continues to argue over whale management schemes, sanctuaries, research interpretations, and illegal whaling, most whale species have been slowly recovering from the brink of extinction, although their future is still uncertain. The IWC now considers some of the whales, such as the Gray Whales, to have reached numbers considered safe. In 2005 researchers estimated the Gray Whale population hovers around eighteen thousand to twenty thousand individuals. However, other whale species, such as the Northern Right and the Bowhead are barely hanging on. The international agreement to protect the whales threatens to be torn apart as the fundamental questions widen and the outcome for the whales becomes more uncertain.

SEVEN

Indigenous Whale Hunting and Whale Watching

The International Whaling Commission (IWC) allows a few aboriginal populations to hunt small numbers of whales. A group is considered aboriginal if their ancestors were the earliest humans to live in a specific area. The IWC recognizes indigenous or aboriginal whaling in only four places: Russia, Greenland, the Caribbean island of Bequia, and the United States. The small number of recognized aboriginal hunts, each with their own limited quotas, add up to only a few hundred whales taken each year, far fewer as a group than those taken illegally and for scientific research by larger countries.

In its efforts to protect endangered whales as well as respect the traditions of indigenous peoples who hunt whales, the IWC requires three conditions be met for indigenous whaling:

- a continuous traditional dependence on whaling;
- both a cultural and nutritional need;
- a noncommercial nature to the hunt and related activities.

Indigenous or aboriginal whaling, even with the conditions set by the IWC, is not easily defined or agreed upon today. There are many ways to interpret "cultural and nutritional need." It is easy to imagine the member countries of the IWC finding much to discuss concerning indigenous whaling.

Only a few indigenous groups truly practice whaling today, based on a millenium of traditional knowledge. For those observing from the outside, it might be hard to see anything traditional in modern methods used by indigenous hunters, including their use of exploding harpoons and powerboats. But if whaling is still a part of the living culture, bridging the past and future, the IWC considers this traditional.

Long before schooners and metal harpoons, the first whalers depended on knowing whales better than what was almost humanly possible. Hunters needed to think like a whale in order to find and kill one. These whale hunters spent their lives studying whale habits and mastering the patience to wait for the whale in a place where one would eventually appear. Whale hunting not only required bravery and strength, but also strict adherence to traditional preparation and procedure, along with a firm belief in supernatural and spiritual intervention. Even then, lives were often lost. For the successful hunter, it was a risk worth taking. One kill might mean a whole season of food for an entire village. It also meant honor for the whaling crew and their families. And if death were the outcome, that too, was an honorable end.

The Inuit of Alaska have never stopped whaling. Their traditions borne of their whale hunting heritage are still a primary part of their social organization and spiritual lives. The Inuit live along the coast of the Arctic Ocean, a world of ice and snow that has made them specialists in the few prey species that live in the far north. The Inuit have survived mostly by hunting Bowhead Whales, seals, and a variety of smaller animals, depending on the season. Their hunt takes place on top of the ice, on the edge of the ice, or in small skiffs. These whale hunters come from a long line of ancestors who have participated in a predator/prey relationship that requires certain skills and knowledge, based on thousands of years of knowledge passed down to each generation.

Inuit whaling teams hunt in small boats, but their weapons have changed as new technologies have become available. Now they use harpoons fitted with brass pipe bombs fired from shoulder guns. Less altered over time are the community harvesting rituals when the hunters kill a whale. The whalers alert the entire Inuit town by radio and the community awaits the long struggle to bring the whale up on the ice for butchering. No one person can own a whale and each person does his or her share of the work, and in turn receives a portion of the food. Community members divide the whale meat according to tradition and they share extra meat with relatives or store it. There is still an entire tradition formed around whaling in this community—a tradition that includes modern technology while keeping the people firmly planted in their past.

From a health perspective, eating whale meat is a growing concern for the Inuit and all cultures who eat whale meat because of studies identifying large amounts of "Persistent Organic Pollutants" or "POPs" throughout the food chain. POPs are described as long-lived chemicals that often travel thousands of miles from point of production or use. POPs build up in the food chain, slowly contaminating fish, animals, and humans. One hot spot for POPs is the Alaskan Arctic where a 1997 study found measurable amounts of chemicals such as DDT, PCBs and hexachlorobenzene (agricultural fungicide) in the blubber of seals, polar bears, and Beluga, Narwhal, and Gray Whales. Tragically, POPs concentrations have also been found in eagles, rabbits, deer, moose, bison, cows, and many other animals.

A Return to Whale Hunting

The Makah Nation is located in the
fishing village of Neah Bay on the Olympic
Peninsula in Washington State. At one time
they had vast areas of coastal territory and
forests. They were skilled mariners and hunters of whales, seals, and salmon, and used
their resources wisely. Whales and whaling

Gray Whale spouting.

ROBIN KOBALY

have always been an integral part of Makah culture, dating back nearly two
thousand years, according to the Makah.

In 1855 the Makah ceded three hundred thousand acres of their
ancestral lands in exchange for maintaining their fishing and whaling
rights. However, the Makah stopped whaling in 1926 due to the depletion
of whales from indiscriminate killing by other whaling nations. This gap
of more than seventy years was long enough for many of the Makah's
time-honored skills and sacred rituals surrounding whaling to be lost. In
the 1990s, some Makah council members reasoned that a return to their
whaling traditions might restore their cultural legacy, give their youth a
sense of pride and dignity, and overall help the Makah to heal spiritually
and physically as a nation. The Makah also believe eating whale and other
sea mammal meat might reverse health problems related to the loss of a
sea-based diet that has been replaced by modern fast food diets.

The Makah's request to resume whaling in 1996 provoked instant
controversy. Using the IWC's decision to remove the Gray Whale from
the Endangered Species List, and the 1855 treaty with the United States,
which secured Makah whale hunting rights, the Makah petitioned to
resume whaling. Their first efforts failed as animal protection organizations filed lawsuits and the National Marine Fisheries Service was taken
to task for not completing an environmental assessment. There were

immediate concerns that by allowing a nation so far removed from its whaling past to once again hunt, the IWC might be opening the floodgates for more commercial whaling.

In *Singing to the Sound: Visions of Nature, Animals & Spirit,* by Brenda Peterson, the author describes the controversial Makah whale hunt and the complex struggles within the Makah nation over whether or not to resume the whale hunt. The Makah Nation was never united in its 1996 quest to return to whaling. Seven Makah elders had protested the hunt, claiming it would be conducted for commercial, not spiritual reasons. "These tribal members believed that the hunters wanted to open the door to a potentially lucrative trade in whale parts with countries such as Japan or Norway," writes Peterson. During the first negotiations, several elders spoke before the IWC to protest the bid, basing their opposition on the fact that it was not a subsistence issue, since no one had eaten or prepared whale meat for at least seventy years. The elders felt that greed was behind the movement and they suggested the whaling proponents had been encouraged by Japanese buyers who promised high prices for whale products.

It was not until the United States attached the Makah's request to that of the Chukotka people of Russia to establish hunting rights and quotas for the whole Eastern Pacific Ocean that the IWC conditionally agreed. Even then the IWC majority was far fewer than usual and commission members attached a clause that stated unlike the Chukotka, the Makah were not officially recognized because their subsistence needs had not been established. While this delayed the hunt, it did not stop it. The IWC gave the Makah permission to hunt twenty whales during the following five years, killing no more than five whales in a given year.

In 1999 the Makah resumed whale hunting and killed one female Gray Whale. They hunted again in 2000, but did not get a whale. As of July 2006 the Makah are waiting for a ruling by the U.S. Federal Appeals Court. Earlier the court ruled that the Makah must comply with the 1972 Marine Mammal Protection Act. The tribe applied for a waiver from that federal act in February 2005. If the Makah receive a waiver they will resume whale hunting.

The reality of the Makah hunting their quota of twenty whales and using the meat seems unrealistic to most critics. If the Makah actually killed five whales in a season, critics question how they could handle more than one hundred thousand pounds of whale meat. Some critics—both from within the Makah nation and outside—believe the Makah would sell the whale meat, most likely to Japan. However, the Makah state unequivocally they would not do this. Those in opposition to the Makah whale hunt say this is not cultural whale hunting, but whaling for commercial profit. However, most of the Makah nation believe their right to continue whale hunting is essential to maintaining their traditional ways.

Behind the scenes pro-whaling nations and many smaller indigenous nations wavering on the issue have paid close attention to the struggle. Offers of millions of dollars have been brokered from both sides of the whaling issue. In 1997 whaling nations established their own organization, World Council of Whalers, and invited several Northwestern tribes to join. The organization quickly declared publicly that indigenous peoples and coastal peoples of Japan and Norway had the right to both hunt and sell whale meat and blubber. The World Council of Whalers lists one hundred delegates, representing nineteen countries.

Celebrating the Whales

Just down the coast from the Makah in La Push, Washington is another nation, the Quileute. A small, federally recognized nation of about seven hundred members, the Quileute ancestors reach back thousands of years. Ancestral lands include a small part of the Olympic Peninsula shoreline and their culture has always been oriented toward the ocean. They have always fished and hunted sea mammals, and were reputedly recognized as the best sealers on the coast. Their red cedar canoes were engineering masterworks and Quileute whaling canoes traveled as far north as Southeast Alaska and as far south as California.

The Quileute have the same treaty rights to hunt whales as the Makah, but they have chosen a different path. Fred Woodruff, tribal elder and member of the Quileute Natural Resources Committee, says, "We choose nature." This approach is in line with the tribe's long tradition of practicing resource management for the benefit of the seventh generation. The Quileute elders state on their website, "Harvesting what is needed for a 'moderate living' and harvesting so enough is left for the future generations, are tribal ways of existence."

Fred Woodruff

Both Gray Whales and Humpback Whales migrate along the shoreline of the Olympic Peninsula. When the Quileute hunted whales they paddled out in their cedar canoes and harpooned as many whales as they needed. For eighty years, the Quileute have not whaled, even though they still hold the treaty rights to hunt whales. "We have chosen instead to honor the whales," Fred explained when asked about this decision.

In 2005 the Quileute received a grant to build a traditional cedar canoe similar to the ones once used by their ancestors. They asked an 82-year-old master carver to go deep into the ancient forest to carefully choose the appropriate cedar tree to create a ceremonial canoe for greeting the whales each spring as they migrate to Arctic

ROBIN KOBALY

Quileute dance at the ceremony for Spirit of Kwalla.

feeding grounds. Over a four-month period Angus Wilson carved a traditional forty-foot canoe to take people out to *watch* whales, not to hunt them.

In a ceremony blessing their new canoe in 2005, Fred prayed, "We focus on our waters. We focus on our timbers. We focus on our animals. We have a lot of good medicine in our hearts that's been handed down to us through the elders of our community. They want these messages to be heard throughout the world." The Quileute's vision is to honor the whales, and during this naming ceremony, they named their canoe *Spirit of Kwalla*, Spirit of the Gray Whale.

The elders have encouraged the young people "to go out and paddle with the whales and share this experience with the public." With the *Spirit of Kwalla*, they are now planning annual whale festivals to build on their ecotourism programs, a major source of income for the Quileute today—and a promising future for the young people.

A new door has been opened between whales and a people who once hunted. Now the Quileute use their traditional canoe, paddles, and ceremonies to celebrate the whales.

EIGHT

Global Warming

*T*he debate over the realities of global warming has continued to heat up in recent years, along with the planet. While some scientists (and many politicians) still contend that global warming is not a threat and is a natural occurrence, the vast majority of scientists agree that significant global warming is already under way, and the urgency to take action increases with every new scientific study. Whether or not the warming of the earth's atmosphere is natural or caused by human activity, the indisputable reality is that it is happening, human pollution adds to the problem, and we must figure out how we are going to stop it.

The Union of Concerned Scientists (UCS), a nonprofit organization of more than one hundred thousand scientists and concerned citizens, identifies global warming as one of the top environmental concerns today. Through the organization's Sound Science Initiative, begun in 1995, thousands of scientists now provide facts on environmental science to respond to and influence fast-breaking media and policy developments on environmental issues of global importance.

The UCS identifies the "fingerprints," or indicators, of global warming as melting glaciers, heat waves, sea-level rise, and Arctic and Antarctic warming. The events that foreshadow global warming include the spread of disease, earlier spring arrival, plant and animal range shifts, coral reef bleaching, downpours, droughts, and fires. Most recently UCS

Central California coastline

scientists provided scientific evidence that links hurricane strength and duration with global warming. "For hurricanes to occur, surface ocean temperatures must exceed 80 degrees Fahrenheit," explained UCS scientists in their report, "Hurricanes and Climate Change." "The warmer the ocean, the greater the potential for stronger storms."

Basically, emissions of carbon dioxide (CO_2) and other heat-trapping gases in the atmosphere cause global warming, impacting all of the earth's major ecological systems, including the oceans. The ability of carbon dioxide and other greenhouse gases to capture radiated heat is one of the reasons life has been able to proliferate on the planet. However, the combination of global clear-cutting of forests and massive burning of fossil fuels has resulted in an astonishing amount of CO_2 that can hang in the atmosphere for decades or even centuries, creating a greenhouse effect.

Scientific studies referred to by the UCS show that carbon dioxide levels in the earth's atmosphere are higher today than they have been for more than four hundred thousand years. Earth's surface temperature has increased measurably over the past one hundred years, and ten of the warmest years on record have occurred since 1990. Scientists say this warming results in changes in rainfall, with some regions becoming wetter and others drier. They predict drought, severe rainfall, and temperature changes worldwide will continue.

In his insightful book, *The Whale and the Supercomputer*, Charles Wohlforth explains another fallout of climate change due to global warming:

> Sea level already has been rising since the last glacial period, when the Bering Sea floor was exposed and connected Alaska with Siberia. Sea level has been much higher in the past, too, as shown by ancient seashores far from the coast in the Arctic and many other places. Climate change accelerates the rise in sea level two ways: water expands when it warms, and melting continental ice increases runoff in the ocean (sea ice does not increase sea level when it melts, because it is already floating in the ocean). In the twentieth century, sea level rose four to eight inches, a rate ten times faster than the average for the previous 3000 years. Rising sea level, with increased erosion, storm damage and flooding, will likely impose costs on many coastal communities. Each area's wealth will determine how it can respond.

Whales and Global Warming

So how does global warming impact whales? Most baleen whales feed on crustaceans such as krill or amphipods in huge concentrations. An adult Gray Whale consumes from 2,000 to 2,500 pounds of amphipods a day when feeding. Whales travel great distances to find these food sources during seasonal migrations that are integral to their other important life processes of mating and birthing. The largest concentrations or swarms of crustaceans are usually found in the more extreme latitudes of both polar regions. Nutrients and vast numbers of ocean organisms worldwide float to the ocean floors where deep, cold ocean currents carry the nutrients and organisms toward the poles. These ocean currents run north and south like huge conveyer belts. When the currents collide with landmasses such as island arcs or continents, the currents carry the nutrients and organisms toward the surface in a process called upwelling. Then sunlight strikes the nutrient-rich surface water causing blooms of sea plants and the organisms who feed upon them.

Nearly all the great whales feed in the cold water of the extreme northern and southern latitudes. If global warming continues, the Pacific Institute for Studies in Development, Environment, and Security predicts "rising temperatures could reduce sea ice by more than 40% in the next century." This could severely deplete the abundance of krill, the primary food source for whales in the Southern Hemisphere. As for the Arctic, the Pacific Institute predicts if the warming trends continue, the region's year-round icepack could be gone within the next fifty years. In turn, this would greatly diminish the phytoplankton population, on which endangered whale species such as Narwhal and Beluga rely.

Global warming could also alter ocean upwelling patterns, resulting in what the Pacific Institute describes as "creating massive blooms of toxins associated with the death of thousands of marine species over the past decade, as well as increasing precipitation in some regions, resulting in the runoff of more pollutants from land into coastal waterways inhabited by whales, dolphins and porpoises." Other marine animals who rely on sea ice, such as polar bears and many species of seals will also be endangered.

One thing is certain: As the planet warms, it affects the systems that regulate climate, some of which are capable of swinging wildly and relatively quickly. The result is increased climate change and more drastic adjustments on a scale we can only imagine. In the meantime, the whales and all of marine life hang in the balance.

NINE

Modern Threats
to Whales

*G*ray Whales faced few threats for many thousands of years as they freely swam the oceans. Orcas, or "killer whales," were their only predator until the advent of whaling. However, within a couple of hundred years the Gray Whales and most other whale species faced the threat of extinction from a new predator—man. By the time the international community halted whaling, the existence of the Pacific Gray Whale, later called the California Gray Whale, hung in the balance, precariously close to extinction. The Atlantic Gray Whale had already been hunted to extinction by 1750.

Since the first efforts to protect the Pacific Gray Whale in 1937, this species has rebounded enough to warrant removal from the endangered species list in 1995—the only large whale to have done so. However, the Gray Whale population in the western Pacific known as Korean Gray Whales are critically endangered. About one hundred Korean Gray Whales remain in 2006. Gray Whales are also the only large whales to have populations that are entirely extinct.

The debate continues over whether or not to resume whale hunting, which is an ongoing threat and could be harmful to the Gray Whales. While that debate continues, all whales face daily threats created by humanity's progress, which could become as devastating to the whales as hunting them. Modern threats include pollution of the oceans, sonar testing, global warming, overfishing, entanglement in fish nets, and collisions with large vessel traffic. What threatens the whales also threatens the overall health of our oceans. In many ways the health of the whales is an indicator of the impending health of the planet.

In 2000 The Pew Charitable Trusts, a nonpartisan, independent research and polling source, funded a special commission to study the world's oceans. The Pew Oceans Commission completed the first national review of the United States' ocean policies since 1969. The three-year review concluded that the world's oceans are in a state of "silent collapse" and cited "human misuse" as the primary cause. The commission represented a wide range of interests, and included eighteen committee members from many walks of life—federal, state, and local elected officials, commercial fishers, scientists, and business leaders.

The commission identified climate change caused by global warming as having a profound impact on the oceans' health in the near future. In addition, the report cited other problems such as pollution, overfishing, aquaculture, coastal development, by-catch waste, habitat alterations, and invasive species. The commission issued a strong warning that the oceans must become a top national priority, recommending the establishment of a National Ocean Policy Act (NOPA) to reformulate national ocean policy that makes healthy marine ecosystems the priority.

While the commission identified major problems with the oceans, it also offered hope if individuals, communities, and nations would work together to make changes. In their final report the commissioners stated, "Our country must articulate a clear, strong commitment to our oceans. As mariners weathered storms for centuries with simple tools, our nation can navigate today's troubled seas. We know what we need: a compass, a chart, and the wind in our sails. That compass is a strong ocean ethic, the chart is a new legal framework, and the wind is our national will. The commitment of leaders and citizens alike is needed to steer us to healthy oceans."

Sonar Testing

Sound is an intricate part of all marine mammals' lives. The toothed whales, such as Orcas and Sperm Whales, have acute echolocation they use to communicate and to find food. Baleen whales, such as Grays, Humpbacks, Blues, and Fins use low-frequency calls that travel over long distances. Whales use sound to communicate with one another, mate, navigate, and most likely achieve other vital purposes in their sea world that we do not know about. Recent findings by whale researchers indicate that whales use sound rather than light to "see" the world around them.

The watery world of whales is filled with competing sounds that can pose problems for whales, especially when navigating, feeding, and communicating. Human-made sounds that pollute the oceans include powerful ship engines, motorboats, air guns, and the potentially deadly military sonar. Imagine whales or dolphins swimming through the seas with this incredible noise pollution.

Of all of these, sonar is the greatest threat. Using a system much like whale echolocation, sonar produces sound waves at low, mid, and high frequencies that penetrate extensive areas of the ocean. The purpose of Military Active Sonar (MAS) is to find other objects in the ocean, especially enemy submarines. The military typically generates over 200 decibels of sonar. In human terms this would be like standing next to a jet at takeoff. Scientific evidence shows that intense blasts of mid-frequency sonar at 235 decibels or more can cause a whale's organs to fatally hemorrhage. The damage reportedly can occur in whales up to twenty miles from the sonar's source.

Dolphins leap in the open sea.

Energy corporations also use sonar and air guns to blast sound waves through the sea floor to detect the presence of oil and gas. Air guns create huge explosions of air underwater much like the depth charges used in World War II. This testing occurs throughout the vast oceans, making it difficult to detect and regulate.

Sonar has been linked to hundreds of whale and dolphin deaths due to stranding, internal bleeding, and stampedes toward the shoreline in desperate attempts to get away from the piercing sonar sound. Scientists believe the intense noise from sonar forces whales to frantically dive or surface, unable to gradually expel the nitrogen in their systems. This causes bubbles in whales' organ tissue from rapid decompression. When they get nitrogen in their blood, this damages internal organs, sensitive hearing membranes, and other vital systems the whales rely on to survive. Whales and humans both from the "bends," or decompression sickness. The reported whale strandings or dead whales washed up on shore likely represent only a portion of the whales and other marine life mortally wounded from sonar. Marine biologists suspect the whales stranded on shore are only the most visible symptom of a problem affecting much larger numbers of marine life. Many scientists believe that blanketing the oceans with sonar's deafening sound could harm entire populations of whales and dolphins.

Even the International Whaling Commission (IWC) has identified sonar as the reason for so many whale strandings, and it has formally protested sonar's continued use. Yet the military, and the oil and gas industries continue to use sonar, ignoring international outcry voiced through the IWC's protests.

In 2003 the Natural Resources Defense Council (NRDC) succeeded in exposing the dangers of active sonar when a federal court ruled as illegal the Navy's plan to deploy Low Frequency Active (LFA) sonar through 75 percent of the world's oceans. Unfortunately, after that court ruling the federal government weakened the court's decision. According to the NRDC, new legislation exempts the U.S. military from core provisions of the Marine Mammal Protection Act—leaving the armed forces much freer to harm whales, dolphins, and other marine mammals in the course of using high-intensity sonar and underwater explosives.

In October 2004 the European Parliament, the elected body of the European Union (EU) representing more than 400 million citizens, approved a resolution to stop deploying high intensity, active naval sonar until more is known about its affect on marine mammals. The European Union's twenty-five member nations, among them Britain, France, Germany, and Spain, approved this resolution, agreeing that sonar poses a significant threat to marine mammals, fish, and other ocean wildlife. The EU's resolution also called for a multinational task force to develop international agreements on sonar and other sources of intense ocean noise. In the interim, the resolution restricts the use of high-intensity, active naval sonar in waters falling under EU jurisdiction. This ruling affects new, low–frequency systems and mid-frequency systems that travel great distances through the oceans.

As the political wrangling over military use of sonar continues, the oceans' inhabitants face ongoing threats. Other impacts, though more subtle, are no less serious. Marine mammals and many species of fish use sound to follow migratory routes, locate each other over great distances, find food, and care for their young. Noise undermines their ability to function and, over the long term, to survive. Naval sonar has been shown to alter the singing of Humpback Whales, an activity essential to the reproduction of this endangered species; to disrupt the feeding of Orcas; and to cause Porpoises and other species to leap from the water, or panic and flee. Over time these sonar effects could slowly undermine the health of sea animal populations, contributing to what prominent biologist Sylvia Earle has called "a death of a thousand cuts."

Polluted Waters

Until recent times humans considered the oceans' bounty to be endless—a blue frontier to use as needed. However, humanity's overuse of ocean resources and a general disregard for the ocean's ecological health have led to numerous environmental crises and long lists of endangered sea life. Sadly, it is not uncommon in 2006 to find posted signs that read, "Beach Closed!"—a warning to heed or else risk serious illness because of polluted waters.

Heal the Bay, a nonprofit group formed in 1985 to monitor California beaches, reported that from April 1, 2004 to March 31, 2005 (364 days) California had a total of 247 separate beach closures. In August 2006, researchers at the University of California, Los Angeles and Stanford University released a study focused on twenty-eight beaches in Los Angeles and Orange Counties in 2000. They found bacterial pollution had sickened as many as one-and-a-half-million swimmers and surfers in that year. Swimming in contaminated water caused symptoms such as stomach cramps, diarrhea, and vomiting. The study did not track ear, nose, and throat problems.

The chief cause of the polluted ocean in Southern California is storm water runoff laden with human and animal waste, pesticides, and oil. This study determined that it would be far less expensive to clean up contaminated water before it reaches the ocean rather than continue to treat millions of sick swimmers annually. Worldwide, the Surfrider Foundation maintains a current list of beaches polluted and/or closed, which adds up to thousands of beach closures annually due to pollution.

A tremendous amount of the ocean's pollution is within three miles of shore, and the worst pollution is often within only a mile of land. We humans have effectively polluted the portion of the ocean that most of us use and love. Coastal waters, including estuaries, lagoons, bays, sloughs, and other inlet features, are incredibly important to coastal ocean life.

Places where rivers and streams enter the ocean are much like ecotones of the land. When wetland features are compromised, untreated waters from gutters, sewers, and other polluted sources enter the oceans without the natural cleansing and settling that nature intended. Storm water is one of the worst pollution agents along populated coastlines globally because it is laced with humanmade debris and microscopic contaminants. This toxic mix overwhelms sewers and gutters, and spills into the oceans and estuaries. More than thirty years after passage of the U.S. Clean Water Act, many of the nation's coastal waters, lakes, and streams are still polluted.

I wonder how it must be for marine life living just offshore from the polluted coastlines. There are no warning signs for them to stay clear of a toxic soup after a rainfall, or to avoid a cruise ship that dumps tens of thousands of gallons of pollution. For whales, dolphins, birds, and other marine life, political and geographical boundaries do not exist. Untreated sewage and toxic waste from industrial plants in one region will mix with cleaner waters from a more ecologically sound region. The result is a huge section of coastline with unclean waters.

For the Gray Whales migrating south back to their home in Baja, most of the Pacific coastline waters are fairly clean. Once the whales reach the waters just above San Francisco and for about the next six hundred to seven hundred miles, well past Ensenada, Mexico, the whales swim through polluted waters. They must travel in ocean waters that would stress the immune system of even the healthiest whales. Only a hundred days later, mother Gray Whales must again swim through these polluted waters with their babies on their northern migration to summer Arctic feeding waters. The unanswered question is how our coastal pollution affects the Gray Whales.

For people living in the Arctic regions, marine mammals are a main source of food. In recent years this traditional food source has become contaminated with the world's pollution. The blubber of marine mammals stores these toxic chemicals, and indigenous peoples eat the blubber and meat. Researchers have found flame-retardant chemicals in high concentrations in Inuit women's breast milk, especially in Nunavik, located in the Arctic region of Quebec. These airborne chemicals, known as polybrominated diphenyl ethers, are found in products such as electronics, computer keyboards, and furniture. Research scientists monitoring this toxic build-up in Inuit women in Nunavik have found that in the past twelve years the presence of these chemicals has increased by 40 percent in their breast milk. These new toxins, persistent organic pollutants (POPs), are in the Arctic environment, transported through the atmosphere. POPs tend to settle in cold regions, where they get into the food chain and concentrate in fatty tissue.

The Arctic Monitoring and Assessment Program, a scientific group funded by Arctic nations, including the United States, issued a report on contaminants in the Arctic, describing the situation as "one of the most serious environmental and human health risks," especially for the Russian Arctic where about two million people live. The report says the sixteen thousand people of Chukotka in northeastern Russia are a main concern because they eat a significant amount of traditional food. The levels of two pesticides, hexachlorobenzene and hexachlorocyclohexane, and, in some areas, PCBs and the pesticide DDT, in Russians are "among the highest reported for all of the Arctic regions." These findings are alarming to Sheila Watt-Cloutier, International Chair of the Inuit Circumpolar Conference, which represents Arctic people in Canada, Alaska, Greenland, and Chukotka. "We are poisoned and so are our children," declared Watt-Cloutier.

Cruise Ship Pollution

Every year more than two hundred cruise ships internationally carry more than ten million passengers across oceans to some of the world's most pristine and beautiful destinations. In 2001 U.S. residents accounted for 82 percent of the industry's global passengers and the number of cruise ships worldwide is expected to double by 2010. The industry is booming, yet hardly anyone who loves cruising has any idea how this kind of vacation impacts oceans and coastlines. Fortunately, environmental groups such as Oceana, a leading nonprofit corporation dedicated to protecting the oceans, are publicizing statistics that make most people pause before making their next vacation a cruise. Based on Environmental Protection Agency

(EPA) estimates, in one week a three-thousand-passenger cruise ship generates about:

- 210,000 gallons of raw sewage;
- 1,000,000 gallons of gray water from shower, sink, and dishwashing water;
- 37,000 gallons of oily bilge water;
- more than 8 tons of solid waste;
- toxic wastes from dry cleaning and photo-processing laboratories;
- millions of gallons of ballast water containing potentially invasive species. Some 7,000 species are transported around the world in ships' ballast water.

The cruise ship industry is building bigger ships capable of carrying five thousand people, so the EPA estimates for pollution will increase considerably with increased passenger load.

Cruise ships can legally dump their raw sewage and toxic waste as close as three miles from shore. Treated sewage, which many consider to be no better than raw sewage, can be dumped anywhere in the ocean—even

Baby elephant seals live on Baja's Cedros Island, located about a mile from a cruise ship lane in the Pacific Ocean.

DOUG THOMPSON

within the three-mile limit—except in marine sanctuaries and in the waters off Alaska.

When Oceana began a campaign to share these practices with cruise passengers, more than 90 percent of the passengers polled wanted cruise ships to upgrade onboard-waste treatment, and 75 percent were against dumping waste *anywhere* in the ocean. Since 2004, Congress has been considering a Clean Cruise Ships Act that proposes prohibiting discharges of any sewage, gray water, or bilge water within twelve miles of U.S. shores or anywhere in the Great Lakes. This proposed legislation will also establish uniform treatment and inspection standards for all cruise discharges. Without public pressure this legislation will languish while cruise ships dump millions of gallons of waste daily.

The second largest U.S. cruise ship company, the Royal Caribbean Cruise Line, decided in May 2004 to install advanced wastewater treatment systems on all of its twenty-nine ships by 2008. This resulted partly from environmental groups' efforts to educate consumers and to rally public opinion to press for change in current cruise practices.

Before you decide on a cruise vacation, ask how the cruise line handles these problems. This is the only way to ensure that the whale or dolphin following your ship is not forced to swim in your toxic waste. Cruise ships depart from the West Coast weekly and travel up and down the Pacific coastline. The whales migrate in their wake. Dolphins, seals, fish, and other marine life live within the pollution these ships create every day.

Overfishing

As of 2005, environmental scientists estimate that 80 to 90 percent of the world's fisheries have been drastically depleted by overfishing. University of British Columbia researchers sounded the alarm in 2001, reporting some fish populations had fallen by as much as 85 percent.

The report noted that use of modern technology helps fishing fleets find marine life hideouts formerly beyond their reach.

In a new book on the problems of overfishing, *Hooked: Pirates, Poaching, and the Perfect Fish,* the author, G. Bruce Knecht warns that the most popular fish populations are less than 10 percent of what they were just fifty years ago. He points to industrial fishing, some of it illegal, as the main reason for this depletion.

According to the United Nations Food and Agriculture Organization (FAO), virtually every commercial fish species in every ocean or sea is listed as "over-exploited," "fully exploited," or "depleted." The FAO warns that nine of the world's seventeen major fishing regions are in serious decline, and production from most of the world's fisheries has reached or exceeds the levels at which fish stocks can regenerate themselves.

Fishing Techniques

This depletion of critical fish stocks took only fifty years due to global commercial fishing fleets that use large-scale and indiscriminate fishing techniques. Long-line fishing, trawls, and gillnets routinely kill non-targeted animals such as sharks, turtles, dolphins, whales, and sea birds. These are referred to as "accidental catch" or "by-catch." Basically, industrial fishing is vacuuming the sea of all but the very smallest of its life forms. This type of fishing is highly wasteful and environmentalists refer to it as "dirty fishing." Every year commercial fishing worldwide wastes more than 16 billion pounds of fish or by-catch and kills hundreds of thousands of marine animals.

Trawling is the most destructive of all fishing methods on the high seas and one that environmentalists are working hard to ban. Trawling threatens whole seamount ecosystems and vast numbers of fish species. Likened to strip mining or clear cutting, trawling indiscriminately destroys ocean

DOUG THOMPSON

Whales are increasingly getting entangled in crab trap gear in the oceans.

habitat, most of which is still unexplored. In addition, trawls destroy corals, sponges, and deep-sea habitats. Fishers set trawls in deep international waters that are not regulated by national laws. This type of dirty fishing results in up to ten pounds of by-catch for every pound of shrimp caught.

Gillnet fishing involves plastic mesh sheets that can easily stretch fifty-miles or more. The goal is to catch thousands of fish by their gills, but this fishing method ends up catching everything in its path. Sea life that is caught but not used is wasted. The Pew Oceans Commission along with other independent studies concluded that an estimated 25 percent of the world's catch is by-catch waste. In addition, nets are left in the water for long periods of time, resulting in unintended additional by-catch such as dolphins and turtles, who end up drowning.

Long-line fishing can extend as far as fifty miles from the boat and have hundreds of baited hooks, primarily for catching tuna, blue and white marlin, and swordfish. However, this method kills about 40,000 sea turtles a year, endangering every species of turtle as well as snagging thousands of sea birds.

Whales are increasingly getting entangled in a jungle of fishing lines and crab traps. They get pulled down by hundreds of pounds of crab traps and bound up in fishing line, which results in drowning. This threat to whales has inspired environmental groups to organize rescue teams of divers willing to cut the ropes and crab traps off the whales. In December 2005 a Humpback Whale just outside the Golden Gate Bridge struggled to stay afloat, hopelessly caught in fishing line and crab traps. A rescue team worked for hours in the water cutting line with curved knives. The whale floated patiently, not threatening the divers' safety. A reporter with the *San Francisco Chronicle* described the freed whale as swimming in what seemed like joyous circles. Then she approached each diver, and nudged each one as if to thank him. The diver who cut the rope out of the whale's mouth said the whale's eye followed his every move—an experience the diver said changed his life.

Government Subsidies

The main reason fishing fleets continue to overfish the oceans is due to government subsidies worldwide. In 1993, the U.N. Food and Agriculture Organization reported that the operating costs of fisheries around the world exceeded commercial revenues by more than $50 billion each year. Worldwide government subsidies allow commercial fishing fleets to continue expanding and adding capacity. More recent estimates show that countries spend about $124 billion annually to catch $70 billion worth of fish. Without subsidies, the world's fishing industry would be bankrupt.

Currently about one percent of the world's oceans are protected. A 2004 study by the World Wildlife Fund (WWF) and Britain's Royal Society for the Protection of Birds estimated that it would actually cost less to protect 30 percent of the world's oceans than it costs to subsidize fishing fleets at current levels. With large protected areas, fisheries might have a chance to recover and sustainable fishing techniques could be put into practice. The oceans' fish stocks are not endless and ocean fisheries and habitats must be allowed to recover.

Aquaculture

Fish farming, or aquaculture, has long been touted as the solution to collapsed fisheries. Already more than one-quarter of the world's seafood comes from aquaculture. Commonly farmed species include shellfish, salmon, and shrimp. Other species such as bluefin tuna are "ranched" or collected from the wild, then penned and fattened before harvesting. Fish farming, as it is usually practiced, does not seem to be a promising way toward the recovery of fisheries or the solution to the world's food shortages. Instead, it stresses local fish populations and ecosystems, and poses a risk to ocean wildlife and human health. For aquaculture to offer a partial solution to diminishing food sources, it will have to be practiced in ways that sustain, rather than deplete, the health of the world's oceans.

Modern salmon farms originated in Norway. They are an updated version of the two-thousand-year-old practice of fish farming in China. Fish farmers selected Atlantic salmon because this fish tolerates captivity relatively well and matures quickly. At first salmon farming seemed like a good solution to the collapse of wild salmon species and it quickly spread to coastlines throughout the world. In British Columbia, Canada, salmon farming seemed a perfect fit. The province soon became North America's biggest producer of farmed salmon.

The problems became apparent after local fishermen noticed the aquaculture farms were usually located in the best areas for wild salmon, threatening the wild stock. One of the biggest concerns with fish farms is that inevitably, farmed fish escape. Soon fishers were catching Atlantic salmon, along with wild Pacific salmon. Already Norway has more farmed Atlantic salmon than its own wild stock in its waters. Environmentalists estimate that in the last decade, more than one million farmed salmon have escaped from farms in British Columbia and Washington State. Atlantic salmon naturally grow much faster than Pacific salmon. These salmon may, in the right conditions, be able to out-compete Pacific salmon, which may include many species of wild salmon already endangered.

Salmon farming is also a problem for marine mammals. Orcas and seals are attracted to the vast numbers of penned fish, and will eat escaped farmed fish. Just as ranchers are allowed to shoot wolves and other cattle killers, fish farmers can protect their salmon from marine mammals like sea lions by shooting them or by driving Orcas away with sonar devices. In many cases whales' and other marine mammals' native feeding grounds compete with salmon fish farming areas.

Farmed salmon are fed pellets of fish meal, fish oil, and slaughterhouse by-products that include blood meal, ground chicken feathers, soybeans, and poultry meal, all mixed with vitamins, minerals, and massive amounts of antibiotics. Farmed salmon require on average at least three pounds of fish meal mixture to every one pound of salmon produced. This is an extremely expensive means to an end, since fisheries are already struggling to provide enough fish to feed fish-farm livestock. The result of this intense feeding and harvesting is high pollution, similar to that found in livestock factory farming. In 2000, fish farms produced the same amount of *daily raw sewage* as a city of one million people!

The antibiotic load of many farmed fish is staggering. Aquaculture farming uses more antibiotics per pound than any type of livestock factory farming, whether on land or sea. Farmed shrimp require massive amounts of antibiotics, which destroy the sensitive habitats where they are raised. It is a common practice worldwide for shrimp farmers to take over and destroy coastal mangrove areas to build shrimp farms. Destruction of mangroves eliminates natural protection for shorelines, especially against hurricanes and sea storms.

Not all the news about fish farming is bad. The farming of bivalves, mussels, clams, and oysters can actually have a positive effect on the environment. They are filter feeders and actually help clean the waters. In addition, they require few chemical additives, do not need fish protein for food, and do not contribute to the collapse of fisheries. Other fish choices that consume less or no protein include tilapia and catfish. Both are less expensive to produce and easier on the environment. Even existing fish farms might run cleaner and more efficiently if they were required to reduce fish density, thereby cutting the need for antibiotics and producing less waste.

In the United States, Europe, and Japan, it is clear these farmed fish are feeding only the wealthiest of the world's peoples. Less production would increase the price, but it would also ensure safer food and a sounder environment. The Marine Stewardship Council (MSC) is a nonprofit, independent global organization established to find solutions to overfishing worldwide. The MSC developed an environmental standard for sustainable and well-managed fisheries. The MSC standard is the only internationally recognized set of environmental principles for measuring sustainable fisheries. The organization now labels products to assure consumers their fish is not caught at the expense of the environment and fisheries. The MSC also lists by country specific stores selling fish products with the MSC label, indicating sustainable fisheries. These fish may cost more, but they are safer for you and the environment. It may take time, but consumer demand wins in the end.

⟶

With more than six billion people on the planet, the global community must work together to protect our land, oceans, and atmosphere. Each of us has a role to play and those of us from wealthy countries have power to influence markets simply by what we choose to buy and eat. If our main criterion is to get the most for the least amount of money, then the environment and animals will suffer. But if we take into account the real cost of eating fish, including the hidden costs to the environment and the welfare of those who made it, then ultimately we can make wiser choices.

There is one prediction I can make: all human-made changes to the environment will change nature, and in turn, all of nature's changes will change us. Every one of our actions concerning the oceans, from overfishing to sonar testing, holds consequences for ocean and human life. Most of the consequences play out slowly, but in the end could be devastating.

Members of the *Haudenosaunee*, or Six Nations Iroquois Confederacy, have a principle in their Great Law of Peace that mandates "in every deliberation we must consider the impact on the seventh generation." In a 1991 interview with Bill Moyers, Chief Oren Lyons of the Turtle Clan of the Onondaga, offered wise counsel for our modern times:

> When you sit in council for the welfare of the people, you council for the welfare of the seventh generation to come so that when their time comes here they may enjoy the same thing that you're enjoying now. I'm sitting here as the seventh generation because seven generations ago, those people were looking out for me.

TEN

Whale Eco-nomics:
A Future with the Whales

One winter day in 1955, fisherman Chuck Chamberlin decided to offer whale-watching trips on his boat to see the Gray Whales as they swam south past San Diego toward Baja. He charged one dollar for the excursion and soon realized people liked the idea of watching whales from a boat. Prior to that first organized boat trip, whale watching took place on shore. The first year several hundred people went whale watching. This was the beginning of what would one day become a multi-billion-dollar industry.

According to Dick Russell in his book, *Eye of the Whale,* marine biologist Raymond M. Gilmore took over Chamberlin's whale watching trips in 1959, and soon had a reputation for leading interesting trips. At that time Gilmore was working with Carl Hubbs on the first aerial counts of Gray Whales in San Ignacio Lagoon, and he was considered one of the experts. Gilmore would later make the bold suggestion to Mexican government officials that they could make more money by whale watching than by whale hunting. Not long after Gilmore popularized the idea of whale watching, other boat captains in Southern California saw the business possibilities and they began offering whale-watching trips. Russell estimates that over the next three years more than four thousand people went whale watching in Southern California.

ROBIN KOBALY

Depoe Bay, Oregon, is a popular spot for watching Gray Whales.

Just as the United States passed the federal Marine Mammal Protection Act and agreed to a worldwide moratorium on whale hunting in 1972, whale watching businesses began to crop up all along the western coast of the United States. The Montreal Zoological Society started Canada's first East Coast whale-watching business in 1971, taking visitors on the St. Lawrence River to see Fin and Beluga Whales. In the late 1970s, whale-watching businesses in New England took off as thousands of tourists became fascinated with Humpback Whales.

By the 1980s and 1990s it was clear that the main attraction in this growing tourist industry—the whales—required little maintenance. As long as the whales had safe passage, they would continue to show up every year and help build up local economies in parts of the world that once struggled to establish livelihoods. San Ignacio Lagoon is an excellent example of how the whale watching industry can provide opportunities in a community with limited economic resources. When economically strapped communities see that whale watching is profitable, they understand the importance of conservation for long-term economic security.

According to Whale and Dolphin Conservation Society (WDCS) Senior Research Fellow, Erich Hoyt, more than nine million people watched whales and dolphins in 1998 and generated more than one billion tourist dollars. Hoyt's estimate for 2000 was nearly eleven-and-a half-million whale watchers who spent almost one-and-a-half billion dollars. Every year the whale-watching industry has grown, bringing new economic life to communities worldwide. In 2004, whale watching in Maui alone attracted almost nine hundred thousand tourists and generated about one billion dollars of business revenue during the five months the Humpback Whales wintered in Hawaiian waters.

In the ongoing debate about whether or not to resume whale hunting, I point out that the profitability of whale watching far exceeds the profitability of whale hunting. For example, a conservative estimate of the value of each of these Humpback Whales looks like this: If three thousand Humpback Whales attract about $700 million in tourist revenue, that would translate into *each* visiting Humpback Whale being worth about $230,000 *annually* to Hawaii. If a Humpback Whale lives at least fifty years, and migrates to Hawaii every other year (at least twenty-five visits in a lifetime), that means one live whale is worth close to $6 million in whale-watching revenue over a lifetime. Female whales are likely to birth many calves over the years, and the flow of revenue will continue. While it is true Hawaii is a high-end tourist area, the tourist revenue will be proportional to any area's economics.

In spring 2005 Japan claimed it made $26.5 million by hunting about a thousand whales in the Antarctic, including Fin Whales. (This report did not factor in the millions of dollars spent by the Japanese government to subsidize the hunt.) At the same time, Japanese conservationists claim that well over one hundred thousand whale watchers in Japan spent more than $30 million in that same year. In the 1990s Japan's booming whale-watching industry—no government subsidies needed—grew at an average rate of 37 percent, according to the Whale and Dolphin Conservation Society.

The Japanese conservation organization, the Dolphin and Whale Action Network (IKAN), along with other Japanese cetacean conservation organizations emphasize that it is "the government, not the people, of Japan who are seeking to liberalize and promote the killing and eating of whales." At the same time, the Japanese government reported that 70 percent of whales killed in 2006 by its whaling fleet in the Antarctic were pregnant. The Japanese government also announced its plans to add Humpback Whales to its whale hunt in 2007.

From a business perspective, I am baffled as to why countries want to continue hunting whales. Whale hunting is not profitable. Like the fishing industries in most countries, governments also subsidize whale hunting. Both the Norwegian and the Japanese governments heavily subsidize their countries' whaling efforts. In addition, Japan also contributes millions of dollars to aid other countries' fishing industries in exchange for their international support of Japan resuming whaling. Critics question why Japan's whaling industry carries so much political and financial clout far beyond its size or popularity. Take away the subsidized money, and there would be no whale hunt. Aside from how one feels about whales, from an economic standpoint it does not make sense.

Even though Norway, Iceland, and Japan continue to hunt whales, all of these countries have large and growing whale-watching industries. Between 1994 and 1998, Iceland had the fastest growing whale-watching industry in the world. In 1991 about one hundred people went whale watching in Iceland; by 2003, there were more than sixty-five thousand whale watchers.

When Iceland resumed whaling in 2003, pro-whaling groups claimed that it was possible to sustain both whale watching and whale hunting. Yet, whale conservationists claim that the friendly, inquisitive whales who approach whale-watching boats would also be the first to be hunted by whalers. This exact scenario played out in July 2006. While about eighty tourists on a whale-watching boat were watching a whale, Norwegian whalers shot and killed the same whale. Norway's newspaper, *Andoyposten,* reported that the whale watchers were "shocked by the slaughter they suddenly and unexpectedly witnessed." On the way back to shore, these same whale watchers saw another Norwegian whaling boat hauling a dead and bloody whale up onto the ship's deck. This most recent incident has made for more troubled waters between whale conservationists and those proposing sustainable whale hunting.

Bottom-line, whales are worth more alive than dead. A whale can only be killed once, but that same whale can be watched many times for many years. The whale-watching industry claims that once it factors in all the benefits to local economies, such as hotels, restaurants, and other tourist amenities, the economic balance weighs firmly on the side of whale watching, not whale hunting.

Many countries such as Brazil, Argentina, and South Africa argue that whale hunting must stop because it will interfere with their profitable whale-watching businesses. Whale watching provides more revenue and more equitable distribution of profits for their countries than would the resumption of commercial whaling. Whale hunters in fleets from far-away developed countries such as Japan kill the whales and take away natural resources from these developing countries.

Whale-watching countries are defending their right to conserve whale resources, and they refuse to relinquish to pressure received from the whaling industry to resume commercial whaling in the oceans near countries promoting whale watching. Aside from Indonesia, no country in the Southern Hemisphere is currently whaling nor intends to start. There are proposals backed by numerous countries in the Southern Hemisphere to permanently forbid whaling south of the Equator. In particular, these countries strongly object to the continuation of

Japanese whaling in the Antarctic. In essence, these countries assert that an outside country that comes into their regions to hunt whales is basically robbing them of their natural resources.

Whale Sanctuaries

Countries worldwide are establishing whale-watching industries, while at the same time designating whale sanctuaries off their coastlines. In 1999, after a decade of lobbying by environmental groups, Italy, France, and Monaco signed a treaty establishing a whale sanctuary off the Italian and French Riviera. Prior to establishing this sanctuary, whale hunting, shipping traffic, and pollution had chased the whales away. Now this area is part of the largest protected area in the Mediterranean—more than 32,400 square miles bordering 1,200 miles of coastline—and it has become a rich resource for whale scientists and local businesses. Their efforts have paid off handsomely. For example, off the coast of Genoa, Italy, one tourist boat can earn up to $300,000 during one summer season of whale watching. Before whale watching, the same boats would earn an average of only $30,000. Genoa has become one of an estimated five hundred communities worldwide now supported by whale watching.

In 1999 Australia established a whale sanctuary that protects all whales and dolphins found in Australian waters. The Australian Whale Sanctuary includes at least forty-five species of whales, dolphins, and porpoises, and has recovery programs for five endangered whale species—Humpback, Blue, Fin, Sei, and Southern Right Whales. Australia has a whale-watching industry estimated to be worth $29 million as of 2003. From 1999 to 2004, the Australian government estimated that its whale-watching industry had grown by 15 percent each year.

Brazil is another good example of a country creating whale sanctuaries while at the same time stimulating the whale-watching business. After an eighteen-month battle with the country's fishing industry, Brazilian environmentalists with the Southern Right Whale Project got Brazil's president to establish a whale sanctuary in 2002. This growing interest in whale conservation sparked a surge in Brazil's whale-watching industry. In addition, the local communities within the sanctuary are beginning to see the benefits of ecotourism and protecting the whales as a part of their livelihood. Brazil and other pro-conservation countries now lead efforts to create a South Atlantic Whale Sanctuary that would reach from the east coast of South America to the west coast of Africa.

Beyond the economics of whales, the world cannot afford to return to whaling. I have spent the past thirty years in close proximity to whales, particularly at San Ignacio Lagoon. During that time I have observed intelligent, gentle whales who care for one another, nurture their young, and peacefully reach out to human beings. Whales have lived on this

Whale watchers on a long-range vessel from San Diego visit with a friendly whale.

ROBIN KOBALY

earth for hundreds of thousands of years. Scientists now believe Gray Whales may live to be more than a hundred years old. There is also a strong possibility that the largest creature to ever inhabit the Earth, the Blue Whale, may live close to two hundred years. Whales are ancient beings who have different forms of intelligence than we do, and if given the opportunity, they can deepen our own knowledge of life. My sense is that they carry knowledge that we humans need in order to survive and thrive. If the whales are endangered, I believe we are in danger.

Whales are capable of inspiring and teaching us during this time of great change if we let them. I am humbled and in awe when I look into the eye of a Gray Whale as she emerges from the swirling gray-blue waters, her heavy eyelids and head almost indistinguishable from the lagoon's water. I would like to think I am capable of holding the whale's gaze, and of learning from her. I realize this is a two-way connection—an interspecies communication.

So, what are they trying to communicate? As the world's environmental problems accelerate, perhaps the whales are trying to let us know how valuable life is. We have enough information about whales and their threatened future to make different decisions from those of our ancestors. When a mother whale brings her precious baby to a boat for the humans to touch, I tell myself, *Perhaps they are trying to communicate to us their value, their intelligence—their absolute right to share the planet with us.*

Resources

Online Resources

The Environmental News Network
www.enn.com
A good source of environmental news worldwide.

The Surfrider Foundation
www.surfrider.org
A grassroots, non-profit, environmental organization that works to protect the oceans and beaches.

National Resources Defense Council (NRDC)
www.nrdc.org
NRDC may be the nation's most effective environmental action organization. They use law, science, and the support of members and online activists to protect wildlife and wild places.

The Whale and Dolphin Conservation Society (WDCS)
www.wdcs.org
WDCS is the global voice for the protection of whales, dolphins, and their environment.

Pew Oceans Commission
www.pewoceans.org
Chartered to assess the condition of America's oceans and living marine resources, and set national priorities to restore and protect them.

Oceana
www.oceana.org
Oceana campaigns to protect and restore the world's oceans, and is a good resource for environmental updates and the latest on the Clean Cruise Ship Act in Congress.

The Ocean Alliance
www.oceanalliance.org
The Ocean Alliance is dedicated to the conservation of whales and their ocean environment through research and education.

The Orca Network
www.orcanetwork.org
Connecting whales and people in the Pacific Northwest

The David Suzuki Foundation
www.davidsuzuki.org
A nonprofit that uses science and education to promote solutions that conserve nature and help achieve sustainability within a generation.

The Environmental Defense
www.environmentaldefense.org
Environmental Defense is a leading national nonprofit that has linked science, economics, and law to create solutions to society's most urgent environmental problems.

The National Oceanic and Atmospheric Administration (NOAA)
www.noaa.gov
NOAA conducts research and gathers data about the global oceans, atmosphere, space, and sun, and applies this knowledge to science.

Green Peace
www.greenpeace.org
A global non-profit organization that focuses on the most crucial worldwide threats to our planet's biodiversity and environment.

The SummerTree Institute
www.summertree.org
The SummerTree Institute provides environmental programs and wildlife ecotourism.

Grist Magazine
www.grist.org
Environmental news and commentary.

Rare Center
www.rareconservation.org
Nature guide training programs that balance business with conservation.

ProPeninsula
www.propeninsula.org
A nonprofit group offering support to organizations throughout the Baja Peninsula. An excellent source of info on the proposed Escalera Nauticá project in Baja.

San Ignacio Lagoon Conservation Fund
www.icfdn.org/campaigns/signacio_whalefund/statusreport.htm
A great resource for understanding indepth efforts to conserve San Ignacio Lagoon and its resources.

WiLDCOAST
www.wildcoast.net
Involved in protecting ecologically important coastal wildlands, islands, and marine areas in California and Baja California. Conservation activities include San Ignacio Lagoon.

Whale Watching Camps of San Ignacio Lagoon

Baja EcoTours
www.bajaecotours. com
Maldo Ficher of San Ignacio Lagoon, and Johnny Friday of La Paz started their base camp in 1989. The SummerTree Institute has teamed up with Baja Ecotours for its five-day expeditions.

Baja Discovery
www.bajadiscovery.com
A San Diego based company owned by Karen Ivey with twenty-five years of expeditions in Baja and San Ignacio Lagoon.

Baja Expeditions
www.bajaex.com
Baja Expeditions is based in La Paz and in San Diego and was founded by Tim Means. Over twenty-five years of leading natural history trips throughout Baja with a base camp in San Ignacio Lagoon since 1991.

Ecoturismo Kuyimá
www.kuyima.com
Kuyimá is owned by members of _Ejido Luis Echeverría,_ who established their two whale watching camps in 1995. Includes a summer program for children through The Kuyimá Center for Environmental Interpretation.

Pachico's Eco Tours
www.pachicosecotours.com
A local owned whale watching camp that is run by Pachico Mayoral and his family. Pachico is credited for having the first friendly encounter with a Gray Whale in San Ignacio Lagoon and was the pioneer of whale watching in San Ignacio Lagoon.

Antonio's Whale Tours
Gerente/Manager: Antonio Aguilar
El Padrino RV Park
San Ignacio Rd, San Ignacio, BCS
Telephone: 011-52-615-154-00-89
Fax 011-52-615-154-02-22
Antonio Aguilar is a lifetime resident of San Ignacio Lagoon who started his whale watching camp after visitors kept knocking on his door asking him to take them out to see the whales.

For more information on Gray Whales visit www.summertree.org

About the Author

 DOUG THOMPSON has spent most of his life as a marine naturalist leading expeditions as well as educational programs to heighten the public's awareness about the perils facing the oceans, marine life, and in particular the whales. As a young man he worked as a commercial fisherman while attending college. It was not unusual for Doug to show up for class with unusual sea specimens tied to the top of his jeep. His lifelong love of the ocean and its creatures resulted in Doug leading more than one hundred long-range natural history expeditions, from Mexico to New Zealand, hosting some of the world's most influential leaders and decision makers.

Doug has also written natural history television programs, including a collaboration with children's entertainer, Sheri Lewis. For many years, he wrote "The Offshore Log," a regular column about the ocean environment, published in California magazines. He is the Director of Expeditions for The SummerTree Institute, a nonprofit environmental education organization. For more than thirty years Doug has led annual expeditions to San Ignacio Lagoon to experience the friendly Gray Whales of Baja. Doug is also the founder of DolphinWorks, providing lectures and natural history experiences for businesses. Doug lives in Southern California with his wife, Robin Kobaly, and their family.

Author's web site: www.dolphinworks.com

About the Photographer

 ROBIN KOBALY has studied and taught the uses of native plants of the Southwest deserts for nearly thirty years. She holds a masters degree in biology, specializing in desert botany. During her twenty-one year career with the U.S. Bureau of Land Management, Robin spent many weeks in helicopters mapping, identifying, and photographing wildlife habitat for the California Desert Conservation Area Plan. She also interpreted aerial photography and satellite imagery to identify plants and wildlife habitat for regional land use management plans. Robin is now the Executive Director of the SummerTree Institute. She has visited San Ignacio Lagoon annually since 1997, photographing the whales, landscape, and people. Robin and Doug have two grown daughters, Holly and Misty, who have traveled with them many times to San Ignacio Lagoon.

Index

Other Books by NewSage Press

NewSage Press has published several books related to the human-animal bond. We hope these books will inspire humanity toward a more compassionate and respectful treatment of all living beings.

Singing to the Sound: Visions of Nature, Animals & Spirit
by Brenda Peterson

Horse Nation: True Stories About Horses and People
by Teresa Tsimmu Martino

Polar Dream: The First Solo Expedition by a Woman and Her Dog
to the Magnetic North Pole
by Helen Thayer

The Wolf, the Woman, the Wilderness: A True Story of Returning Home
by Teresa Tsimmu Martino

Blessing the Bridge: What Animals Teach Us About Death,
Dying, and Beyond
by Rita Reynolds

Three Cats, Two Dogs, One Journey Through Multiple Pet Loss
by David Congalton

Conversations with Animals: Cherished Messages and Memories
as Told by an Animal Communicator
by Lydia Hiby with Bonnie Weintraub

Food Pets Die For: Shocking Facts About Pet Food
By Ann N. Martin

Protect Your Pet: More Shocking Facts
by Ann N. Martin

Pets at Risk: From Allergies to Cancer, Remedies for an
Unsuspected Epidemic
By Alfred J. Plechner, DVM with Martin Zucker

NEWSAGE
PRESS

NewSage Press
PO Box 607, Troutdale, OR 97060-0607

Phone Toll Free 877-695-2211; Fax 503-695-5406
Email: info@newsagepress.com
Distributed to bookstores by Publishers Group West
800-788-3123 (U.S.) or 416-934-9900 (Canada)